Slow Cooker Favorites

SOUPS, STEWS, and CHILIS

150+ EASY, DELICIOUS SLOW COOKER RECIPES,
from Cincinnati Chili and Beef Stew to Chicken Tortilla Soup

Adams Media
New York London Toronto Sydney New Delhi

Adams Media
An Imprint of Simon & Schuster, Inc.
57 Littlefield Street
Avon, Massachusetts 02322

First Adams Media trade paperback edition OCTOBER 2017

ADAMS MEDIA and colophon are trademarks of Simon and Schuster.

For information about special discounts for bulk purchases, please contact Simon & Schuster Special Sales at 1-866-506-1949 or business@simonandschuster.com.

The Simon & Schuster Speakers Bureau can bring authors to your live event. For more information or to book an event contact the Simon & Schuster Speakers Bureau at 1-866-248-3049 or visit our website at www.simonspeakers.com.

Interior design by Colleen Cunningham

Manufactured in the United States of America

10 9 8 7 6 5 4 3

Library of Congress Cataloging-in-Publication Data has been applied for.

ISBN 978-1-5072-0503-7
ISBN 978-1-5072-0504-4 (ebook)

Many of the designations used by manufacturers and sellers to distinguish their products are claimed as trademarks. Where those designations appear in this book and Simon & Schuster, Inc., was aware of a trademark claim, the designations have been printed with initial capital letters.

Always follow safety and comonsense cooking protocols while using kitchen utensils, operating ovens and stoves, and handling uncooked food. If children are assisting in the preparation of any recipe, they should always be supervised by an adult.

Contains material adapted from the following titles published by Adams Media, an Imprint of Simon & Schuster, Inc.: *The Everything® Healthy Slow Cooker Cookbook* by Rachel Rappaport with B.E. Horton, MS, RD, copyright © 2010, ISBN 978-1-4405-0231-6; *The Everything® Mediterranean Slow Cooker Cookbook* by Brooke McLay and Launie Kettler, copyright © 2014, ISBN 978-1-4405-6852-7; *The Everything® Vegan Slow Cooker Cookbook* by Amy Snyder and Justin Snyder, copyright © 2012, ISBN 978-1-4405-4407-1; *The Everything® Vegetarian Slow Cooker Cookbook* by Amy Snyder and Justin Snyder, copyright © 2012, ISBN 978-1-4405-2858-3; *The Everything® Slow Cooker Cookbook, 2nd Edition* by Pamela Rice Hahn, copyright © 2009, ISBN 978-1-59869-977-7; *The Everything® Gluten-Free Slow Cooker Cookbook* by Carrie S. Forbes, copyright © 2012, ISBN 978-1-4405-3366-2; and *The Everything® Indian Slow Cooker Cookbook* by Prerna Singh, copyright © 2012, ISBN 978-1-4405-4168-1.

Contents

Introduction

Are you sick of cleaning up a mountain of dirty dishes? Looking to serve a crowd? Does the simple act of eating a home-cooked meal seem like a luxury?

If this sounds familiar, it's time for you to plug in your slow cooker and make a hot meal a priority—not a chore.

With a slow cooker, you can create everything from appetizers to soups and stews to flavorful entrées and you don't have to worry about spending hours—or much time at all—in the kitchen. Just drop in your ingredients, turn on the slow cooker, and you're out the door with a delicious dinner guaranteed to greet you when you get home.

In *Slow Cooker Favorites: Soups, Stews, and Chilis*, you'll find more than 150 warming slow cooker recipes that make dinnertime easy, inexpensive, and incredibly versatile. These flavor-packed dishes come from a variety of cuisines—Mediterranean, Italian, Asian, and Indian—and we even serve up a number of American favorites like Texas Firehouse Chili, Simple Split Pea Soup, and Basic Beef Stew. You'll also find a chapter that gives you the rundown on how to use, clean, and store your slow cooker and information on how to customize your recipes once you get the hang of using this appliance.

So whether you're craving Smoky Chipotle Pork Chili; Garden Vegetable Soup; Ham, Cabbage, and Carrot Stew; or just some good old Minestrone Soup; with *Slow Cooker Favorites: Soups, Stews, and Chilis* you'll always know what's for dinner.

CHAPTER 1

Slow Cooker Basics

So you know you want to use a slow cooker and you're excited to whip up the delicious soups, stews, and chilis found throughout the book. But, where do you start? In this chapter, you'll learn everything you need to know to choose, cook with, clean, and store your slow cooker. In addition, you'll find some basic techniques for using this appliance as well as some info on the methods and terminology used in the book to make cooking with your slow cooker as easy as possible. Let's get cooking!

What Slow Cooker Equipment Should You Buy?

Maybe you've gone to buy a slow cooker and were intimidated by all the options. It can be intimidating. With so many different styles from which to choose, how do you pick the one that's right for you?

There are small 1-quart versions that are perfect for hot-dip appetizers and large 8-quart models that make enough stew for a large family. There are versions with automatic timers and warming settings. Some have removable crockery inserts, while others have the crock built into the device.

The first thing you need to do is take a look at how you'll be using the device. Are you routinely gone for more than nine hours during the day? If so, you might want to consider the automatic timer and warming functions because even a slow cooker can overcook some food. Do you want to make entire meals? The two-compartment model would provide more options. If you don't like to spend a lot of time washing pots and pans, consider a slow cooker with a removable crockery insert. These can be cleaned in the dishwasher, while self-contained units must be sponge cleaned. The good news is that a slow cooker remains a slow cooker. It's a relatively simple device that's hard to use incorrectly.

If you are lucky enough to plan your purchase of a slow cooker, define what you will be using it for. Do you have more than four people in your family? If so, you might want to go with a 6-quart or even 8-quart version. Someone who does a lot of entertaining or likes to freeze leftovers might want the larger version. Many of the recipes throughout this book call for either a 4- or a 6-quart slow cooker, so keep that in mind while choosing your appliance. Once you decide what type of slow cooker to buy, you'll need to figure out how to use it. Read on…

How to Use Your Slow Cooker

Today's slow cookers usually have two settings—high and low. The low setting is equivalent to about 200°F at its highest, while the high setting gets up to about 300°F. However, the reason they are listed as high and low is because the actual degrees don't matter. Since the food heats indirectly, absorbing the heat from the crockery, it will cook the same way within a 50-degree temperature range.

Slow cookers heat up slowly, usually taking two to three hours to get up to their highest temperature. This ensures that the food retains its nutrients while also preventing scorching or burning. It's also the reason you don't need to be home while the meal cooks. When your slow cooker is on, resist the urge to lift the cover to view, smell, or stir the contents. Every time you lift the cover of the slow cooker, valuable steam escapes, reducing the internal temperature several degrees. This steam that the slow cooker creates is an important factor in creating those marvelous flavors—foods are cooked in their own steam, literally infusing the flavor back in through the cooking process. This keeps the food moist and works to tenderize the meat and even the most stubborn vegetables. Every time you lift the cover, plan to add at least twenty minutes to your cooking time.

Slow Cooker Suggestions

The heating elements for a slow cooker are across the bottom of the slow cooker and up the sides. Until you become very familiar with the quirks of your slow cooker, cooking on low is the safest bet for ensuring the food turns out the way you want it.

Even the most inexperienced cook can quickly master slow cooker recipes. Just keep the following things in mind:

- Cut meat and vegetables to the same size to ensure even cooking in soups and stews.
- Place slow-cooking items such as hard vegetables—rutabagas, turnips, potatoes—on the bottom of the slow cooker.
- Slow cooker recipes don't like water. Because the food is infused with steam, very little water escapes. When converting a recipe from a regular cookbook, use about half the water and add more during the last hour of the cooking cycle if necessary.

- Most traditional slow cooker recipes take seven to nine hours on the low setting. The high setting takes about half that time but doesn't tenderize the meat as much.
- Spices and aromatic vegetables have different characteristics when slow cooked. Some, such as green peppers and bay leaves, increase in intensity when slow cooked. Others, such as onions and cinnamon, tend to lose flavor over the long cooking process. Most slow cooker recipes reflect this difference, although you may have to adjust for your own tastes.
- When cooking traditional slow cooker meals such as soups, stews, and meats, make sure the slow cooker is at least half full and the food does not extend beyond 1" below the top. This ensures even cooking.
- Don't thaw food in the slow cooker. While it may seem a natural use, frozen food actually heats up too slowly to effectively prevent bacterial growth when in a slow cooker. It's better to thaw food overnight in a refrigerator or use the microwave.

With these things in mind, you'll be a slow cooker professional before you know it.

How to Care for Your Slow Cooker

Slow cookers are very simple appliances. However, they do need some special care. If you follow these rules your slow cooker will produce healthy meals for many years:

- Never, never, never immerse the slow cooker in water. If it's plugged in at the time, you could receive a shock. If it isn't plugged in, you could damage the heating element.
- Always check for nicks or cuts in the electrical cord before plugging it into the outlet. This is especially important because you may be leaving the slow cooker on for several hours with no one in the house.
- Parts of the slow cooker can be cleaned in a dishwasher. If you have a removable crockery core, place it on the bottom rack. If you have a

plastic cover, be sure to place it in the top rack of the dishwasher so it doesn't warp. If the crockery container isn't removable, simply use a soft cloth or sponge to wash it out. Always use a damp cloth to wash the metal housing.

- Remove baked-on food from the crockery container with a nonabrasive cleaner and a damp sponge. Do not scrub with abrasives, as these can scratch the crock, creating areas for bacteria to reside.

Be sure to follow all of these rules to guarantee your slow cooker will both last for many years and perform at maximum potential with each use.

Slow Cooker Suggestions

Cooking with a slow cooker becomes even easier when you use slow cooker liners. The liners are made of food-safe, heat-resistant nylon. They also make slow cooker cleanup fast and easy because you simply place the liner in the slow cooker crock, add the ingredients, cook according to the recipe instructions, throw the liner away when you're done, and wipe down the slow cooker and wash the lid.

What Else Do You Need to Know?

So now you know how to buy, cook with, and clean your slow cooker. Now let's take a look at what else you need to know to successfully make the deliciously easy meals found throughout the following recipes chapters.

Learn Some Cooking Terms

Throughout this book, you'll encounter cooking terms usually associated with other methods of cooking. While the slow cooker does provide an easy way to cook foods, there are simple tricks you can use to let your slow cooker mimic those other methods. Cooking methods terms you'll find in this book include the following:

- **Baking** usually involves putting the food that's in a baking pan or ovenproof casserole dish in a preheated oven; the food cooks by being surrounded by the hot, dry air of your oven. (In the case of a convection oven, it cooks by being surrounded by circulating hot, dry air.) In the slow cooker, food can be steam-baked in the cooker itself, or you can mimic the effect of baking at a low oven temperature by putting the food in a baking dish and resting that dish on a cooking insert or rack.

- **Braising** usually starts by browning meat in a skillet on top of the stove and then putting the meat with a small amount of liquid in a pan with a lid or covering and slowly cooking it. Braising can take place on the stovetop, in the oven, or in a slow cooker. The slow-cooking process tenderizes the meat. Incidentally, the liquid that's in the pan after you've braised meat often can be used to make a flavorful sauce or gravy.

- **Sautéing** is the method of quickly cooking small or thin pieces of food in some oil or butter that has been brought to temperature in a sauté pan over medium to medium-high heat. Alternatively, you can sauté in a good-quality nonstick pan without using added fat; instead use a little broth, nonstick cooking spray, or water in place of the oil or butter. As mentioned later in this chapter, another alternative is to steam-sauté food in the microwave.

- **Stewing** is similar to braising in that food is slowly cooked in a liquid; however, stewing involves a larger liquid-to-food ratio. In other words, you use far more liquid when you're stewing food. It is the method often associated with recipes for the slow cooker. Not surprising, this method is most often used to make stew.

Make Each Dish Your Own

Throughout this book you'll find suggestions for how you can take shortcuts or add a bit of additional personality to a dish without compromising the recipe. Straying from the recipe may seem scary at first, but once you understand the logic behind such shortcuts, you'll begin to look at them as alternative measures rather than total improvisations. Before you know it, you'll be adding a little bit of this and a little bit of that with the best of them. For example:

- **Use broth bases or homemade broth:** Use of a broth base or home-made broth lets you eliminate the need to stir-fry meat and sauté vegetables. In addition, broth bases can be made double strength, which saves you the time of reducing broth and you avoid that briny, overly salty taste associated with bouillon cubes. Bases also take up less storage space. It usually only takes ¾ to 1 teaspoon of broth mixed together with a cup of water to make 1 cup of broth. A 16-ounce container of base, for example, is enough to make 6 gallons of broth.

- **Use a microwave-safe measuring cup:** Rather than dirtying a microwave-safe bowl and a measuring cup, planning the steps so that you add the ingredients to a microwave-safe measuring cup means you can use it to sauté or steam onions or other vegetables called for in the recipe. This makes it easier to pour the results into the slow cooker and you end up with fewer dishes to wash.

- **Steam-sauté vegetables in the microwave:** Sautéing vegetables in the microwave has the added advantage of using less oil than it would take to sauté them in a pan. Or you can compromise further and eliminate the oil entirely and substitute broth if you prefer. Just because a recipe suggests sautéing the onions in a nonstick skillet doesn't mean that you can't use the alternative microwave method, or vice versa. Use the method that is most convenient for you. On the other hand, skipping other steps, like sautéing onion, carrot, celery, or bell pepper before you add them to the slow cooker, won't ruin the taste of the food; you'll just end up with a dish that tastes good instead of great. When time is an issue, there may be times when good is good enough. And that's okay.

- **Take advantage of ways to enhance or correct the flavor:** Like salt, a little bit of sugar can act as a flavor enhancer. The sweetness of sugar, honey, applesauce, or jelly can also be used to help tame an overly hot spicy dish or curry. Just start out adding a little bit at a time; you want to adjust the flavor without ending up with a dish with a cloying result.

- **Use fresh herbs:** There are other times you may need to adjust some of the recipe instructions. For example, if you have fresh herbs on hand, it's almost always better to use those instead of dried seasoning;

however, if you substitute fresh herbs, don't add them until near the end of the cooking time. Also keep in mind that you need to use three times the amount called for in the recipe. In other words, if the recipe specifies 1 teaspoon of dried thyme, you'd add 1 tablespoon (3 teaspoons) of fresh thyme.

- **Use frozen, not fresh:** If you're using frozen meat to replace the raw meat called for in the recipe, chances are you can add it straight from the freezer to the slow cooker and not greatly affect the cooking time. If the meat is thawed, you'll want to wait until near the end of the cooking time to add it so that you don't overcook the meat.

Again, if you're nervous or just aren't comfortable cooking with a slow cooker yet, don't worry. Follow the recipes throughout the book, learn what you like and what you don't like, and then take the next step. The possibilities are endless!

CHAPTER 2

Broths, Stocks, and Creams

No-Beef Broth

YIELDS

4 C

4 medium carrots, scrubbed and cut into large pieces

2 large onions, peeled and quartered

1 celery stalk, chopped

2 cups sliced fresh portobello mushrooms

1 whole bulb garlic, crushed

1 tablespoon vegan Worcestershire sauce

1 tablespoon brown sugar

6 cups water

1. In a 4-quart slow cooker, add all ingredients; cover and cook on low heat for 8–10 hours.
2. Strain the broth to remove the vegetables. Store in a covered container in the refrigerator for 2–3 days or freeze for up to 3 months.

Vegetable Stock

YIELDS

4 C

2 large onions, peeled and halved

2 medium carrots, scrubbed and cut into large pieces

3 celery stalks, cut in half

1 whole bulb garlic, crushed

10 black peppercorns

1 dried bay leaf

6 cups water

1. In a 4-quart slow cooker, add all ingredients; cover and cook on low heat for 8–10 hours.
2. Strain the broth to remove the vegetables. Store in the refrigerator.

Slow Cooker Suggestions

Homemade broth can be stored in a covered container in the refrigerator for 2–3 days or frozen for up to 3 months.

Roasted Chicken Broth

Bones from 1 whole chicken carcass

1 large onion, peeled and quartered

2 celery stalks, chopped

3 large carrots, unpeeled, chopped

1 tablespoon olive oil

8½ cups water

1 bunch fresh flat-leaf parsley sprigs, chopped

1 bunch fresh dill sprigs

1 tablespoon sea salt

1 teaspoon black peppercorns

1. Preheat oven to 350°F.
2. Place chicken bones, onion, celery, and carrots on a large rimmed sheet pan. Drizzle with olive oil and roast for 1 hour.
3. Place bones and vegetables in a 6-quart slow cooker and add the water. Add the parsley, dill, salt, and pepper.
4. Cook on low for 8 hours.
5. Strain the broth through a colander and discard the solids. Store in the refrigerator for 3 days or freeze for up to 2 months.

Slow Cooker Suggestions

Roasting chicken bones along with vegetables helps to create a darker and richer broth. However, when using a broth for soup remember that clear broths are better for delicate dishes, and roasted broths are better for hearty dishes.

Pork Broth

1 (3-pound) bone-in pork butt roast
1 large onion, peeled and quartered
12 baby carrots
2 celery stalks, cut in half
4½ cups water

1. Add all the ingredients to a 4-quart slow cooker. Cover and cook on low for 6 hours or until the pork is tender and pulls away from the bone.
2. Strain; discard the celery and onion. Reserve the pork roast and carrots for another use. Once cooled, cover and refrigerate the broth overnight. Remove and discard the hardened fat. The broth can be kept for 1–2 days in the refrigerator or frozen for up to 3 months.

Slow Cooker Suggestions

To make concentrated broth and a pork roast dinner at the same time, increase the amount of carrots, decrease the water to 2 cups, and add 4 peeled, medium sweet potatoes (cut in half) on top. Cook on low for 6 hours.

Chicken Stock

1 (7-pound) chicken carcass

2 large carrots, peeled and cut into chunks

2 celery stalks, cut into chunks

2 medium onions, peeled and cut into chunks

2 parsnips, cut into chunks

1 head garlic

2 chicken wings

Water, as needed

1. Place the carcass, carrots, celery, onions, parsnips, garlic, and wings into a 6-quart slow cooker.
2. Fill the slow cooker with water until it is 2" below the top. Cover and cook on low for 10 hours.
3. Strain into a large container. Discard the solids. Refrigerate the stock overnight.
4. The next day, scoop off any fat that has floated to the top. Discard the fat.
5. Freeze or refrigerate the stock and use within 1 week.

Slow Cooker Suggestions

Any leftover vegetables can be added to stock for extra flavor; fennel fronds, green onions, turnips, and red onion are all good choices. Depending on the recipe that the stock will be used in, adding items like dried chilies, ginger, or galangal root will customize the stock, making it an even better fit for the final product.

Turkey Stock

1 pound celery, chopped, leaves reserved

1 small turkey carcass

1½ pounds yellow or red onions, peeled and quartered

½ pound carrots, peeled and chopped

½ pound parsnips, peeled and chopped

¼ pound shallots, peeled and halved

1 bunch fresh flat-leaf parsley sprigs

4 sprigs fresh thyme

1 sprig fresh rosemary

1½ gallons water

2 dried bay leaves

20 black peppercorns

1. Set aside celery leaves and place all other ingredients in a 6-quart slow cooker. Cover and cook on low for 7½ hours.

2. Add celery leaves and cook for 30 minutes longer.

3. Strain the stock and discard the solids. Refrigerate at least 2 hours. Skim the fat that solidifies at the surface before using or freezing. Freeze for up to 3 months.

Beef Stock

YIELDS

2 QT

8 black peppercorns

5 sage leaves, fresh

4 large onions, peeled and thickly sliced

4 medium carrots, thickly sliced

4 small celery stalks, thickly sliced

2½ quarts water

2 ribs from cooked beef rib roast, fat trimmed

2 bay leaves, dried

1 parsnip, peeled and sliced

1. Combine all the ingredients in a 6-quart slow cooker. Cover and cook on low for 6–8 hours.
2. Strain the stock through a double layer of cheesecloth, discarding the solids.
3. Refrigerate 2–3 hours, until chilled. Remove fat from the surface of the stock.
4. Freeze or refrigerate the stock and use within 1 week.

Fish Stock

2 pounds cooked fish bones

1 pound shrimp shells

1 pound red or white onions, peeled and quartered

1 pound celery stalks, chopped

1 pound carrots, peeled and chopped

1 bunch fresh flat-leaf parsley sprigs

1 leek, chopped

2 garlic cloves, peeled and halved

1 large fennel bulb, quartered

2 tablespoons dry white wine

1½ gallons water

10 black peppercorns

1. Place all ingredients in the slow cooker. Cover and cook on low for 5 hours.

2. Strain the stock and discard the solids. Refrigerate at least 2 hours. Skim the fat that solidifies at the surface before using or freezing. Freeze for up to 3 months.

Slow Cooker Suggestions

Whenever you cook seafood, toss the bones and shells in a plastic bag and freeze them until you're ready to make stock. A varied collection of bones and shells will result in an even more delicious stock.

Seafood Stock

YIELDS 4 C

2 pounds large or jumbo shrimp, crab, or lobster shells

1 large onion, peeled and thinly sliced

1 tablespoon fresh lemon juice

4 cups water

1. Add the seafood shells, onion, lemon juice, and water to a 4-quart slow cooker. Cover and cook on low for 4–8 hours.
2. Strain through a fine sieve or fine wire-mesh strainer. Discard the shells and onions. Refrigerate in a covered container and use within 2 days or freeze for up to 3 months.

Slow Cooker Suggestions

For each cup of seafood or fish stock called for in a recipe, you can substitute ¼ cup of bottled clam juice and ¼ cup of water. Just keep in mind that the clam juice is very salty, so adjust any recipe in which you use it accordingly.

Brown Stock

2 large carrots, scrubbed

2 celery stalks

1 (1½-pound) bone-in chuck roast

1½ pounds cracked beef bones

1 large onion, peeled and quartered

¼ teaspoon freshly ground black pepper

4½ cups water

1. Preheat the oven to 450°F. Cut the carrots and celery into large pieces. Put them, along with the meat, bones, and onions, into a roasting pan. Season with pepper. Put the pan in the middle part of the oven and, turning the meat and vegetables occasionally, roast for 45 minutes or until evenly browned.

2. Transfer the roasted meat, bones, and vegetables to a 4–6-quart slow cooker. Add the water to the roasting pan; scrape any browned bits clinging to the pan and then pour the water into the slow cooker. Cover and cook on low for 8 hours. (It may be necessary to skim accumulated fat and scum from the top of the pan juices; check the broth after 4, and again after 6, hours to see if that's needed.)

3. Use a slotted spoon to remove the roast and beef bones. Reserve the roast and the meat removed from the bones for another use; discard the bones.

4. Once the broth has cooled enough to handle, strain it; discard the cooked vegetables. Refrigerate the (cooled) broth overnight. Remove and discard the hardened fat. The resulting concentrated broth can be kept for 1–2 days in the refrigerator, or frozen for up to 3 months.

Roasted Vegetable Stock

YIELDS

4 QT

3 large carrots, peeled

3 large parsnips, peeled

3 large onions, peeled and quartered

3 whole turnips

3 medium rutabagas, quartered

3 medium bell peppers, halved and seeded

2 medium shallots, peeled

1 whole head garlic

1 bunch fresh thyme sprigs

1 bunch fresh parsley sprigs

3½ quarts water

1. Preheat oven to 425°F. Arrange the vegetables and herbs in a 9" × 13" baking pan lined with parchment paper. Roast for 30 minutes or until browned.

2. Transfer the vegetables to a 4–5-quart slow cooker. Add water and cover. Cook on low for 8–10 hours. Strain the stock, discarding the solids. Freeze or refrigerate the stock until ready to use.

Savory Vegetable Stock

YIELDS

2 pounds yellow onions, peeled and quartered

1 pound carrots, scrubbed, unpeeled, and chopped

1 pound celery, chopped

½ pound button mushrooms, cleaned and halved

1 bunch fresh parsley sprigs

1 bunch fresh dill sprigs

4 sprigs fresh thyme

10 cups water

2 bay leaves (fresh or dried)

1 tablespoon sea salt

20 black peppercorns

1. Place all ingredients in a 4–5-quart slow cooker and cook on low for 8 hours.
2. Remove the solids with a slotted spoon and discard. Refrigerate for up to 3 days or freeze and store for up to 3 months.

Mushroom Stock

YIELDS

1 quart water

12 ounces white mushrooms

6 sprigs fresh parsley

1 large onion, peeled and sliced

1 leek (white part only), chopped

1 celery stalk, sliced

2 ounces dried shiitake mushrooms

1 tablespoon minced garlic

1½ teaspoons black peppercorns

¾ teaspoon dried sage

¾ teaspoon dried thyme

¼ teaspoon freshly ground black pepper

1. Combine all the ingredients except pepper in a 6-quart slow cooker; cover and cook on low for 6–8 hours.
2. Strain, discarding solids; season with pepper. Serve immediately, refrigerate and use within 1–2 weeks, or freeze.

White Wine Vegetable Stock

YIELDS

1 G

1½ teaspoons olive oil

1½ pounds yellow or red onions, peeled and quartered

¼ pound shallots, peeled and halved

1 large leek, chopped

½ pound carrots, peeled and chopped

1 pound celery, chopped, leaves reserved

1 cup Pinot Grigio (or other light white wine)

1½ gallons water

1 bunch fresh parsley sprigs

4 sprigs fresh thyme

2 bay leaves (fresh or dried)

20 black peppercorns

1. Heat the olive oil in a Dutch oven over medium heat. Add the onions, shallots, leek, carrots, and celery. Sauté until vegetables have softened, 5–8 minutes. Pour in the wine and cook for 5 minutes, until slightly reduced.

2. Transfer the vegetable mixture to a 4–5-quart slow cooker. Add water.

3. Stir in parsley, thyme, bay leaves, and peppercorns, and cook on low heat for 7½ hours. Add celery leaves, and cook for an additional 30 minutes.

4. Strain the stock, discarding the solids. Freeze or refrigerate the stock until ready to use.

Slow Cooker Suggestions

Celery leaves can be an overlooked ingredient. They can be dried and mixed with kosher salt to create your own celery salt, which adds a fresh flavor to soups, stews, and sauces. Also, fresh chopped celery leaves are wonderful to use as a final step to finish dishes.

Red Wine and Tomato Vegetable Stock

YIELDS

1 G

½ pound tomatoes

1½ teaspoons olive oil

1½ pounds yellow onions, peeled and quartered

¼ pound shallots, peeled and halved

½ pound carrots, peeled and chopped

1 pound celery, chopped

½ pound portobello mushrooms, chopped

4 cloves garlic, peeled and chopped

1 cup dry red wine

1½ gallons water

1 bunch fresh parsley sprigs

4 sprigs fresh thyme

2 bay leaves (fresh or dried)

20 black peppercorns

1. Bring a large pot of water to a boil. Fill a large bowl with cold water and ice. Gently cut a small "×" in the bottom of each tomato, just piercing the skin. Place tomatoes one at a time on a slotted spoon and gently drop into the boiling water. Repeat until all tomatoes are in the pot. Cook the tomatoes for 1 minute and remove with the slotted spoon. Place the tomatoes in the ice bath to cool. Remove skins of tomatoes when cooled, and roughly chop.

2. Heat the olive oil in a Dutch oven over medium heat. Add the onions, shallots, carrots, and celery. Sauté until softened, 5–8 minutes. Add the tomatoes, mushrooms, and garlic. Stir for 1 minute.

3. Pour in the wine and cook until almost completely evaporated, about 10 minutes.

4. Transfer the vegetable mixture to a 4–5-quart slow cooker and add water. Stir in parsley, thyme, bay leaves, and peppercorns and cook on low for 8 hours.

5. Strain the stock, discarding the solids. Freeze or refrigerate the stock until ready to use.

Cream of Broccoli Soup

SERVES 4

1 (12-ounce) bag frozen broccoli florets, thawed

1 small onion, peeled and diced

4 cups chicken broth

¼ teaspoon salt

¼ teaspoon freshly ground black pepper

4 slices white bread, crusts removed

1 cup heavy cream

1. Add the broccoli, onion, broth, salt, and pepper to the slow cooker; cover and cook on low for 4 hours. Tear the bread into pieces and stir them into the broth.

2. Use an immersion blender to purée the soup. Stir in the cream. Cover and, stirring occasionally to ensure that the bread remains blended in with the soup, cook on low for 30 minutes or until the soup is brought to temperature.

Cream of Mushroom Soup

SERVES 4

8 ounces fresh mushrooms, cleaned and sliced

1 small onion, peeled and diced

4 cups chicken broth

¼ teaspoon salt

¼ teaspoon freshly ground black pepper

1 cup heavy cream or crème fraîche

1. Add the mushrooms, onion, broth, salt, and pepper to the slow cooker; cover and cook on low for 4 hours.

2. To purée the cooked diced onion, first use a slotted spoon to remove some of the mushrooms and set aside. Use an immersion blender to purée and then return the reserved mushrooms to the slow cooker.

3. Stir in the cream or crème fraîche. Cover and cook on low for 30 minutes or until the soup is brought to temperature.

Cream of Winter Vegetables Soup

2 tablespoons butter

4 leeks

1 large yellow onion, peeled and diced

4 medium carrots, peeled and sliced

4 medium potatoes, peeled and diced

2 large turnips, peeled and diced

6 cups boiling water or chicken broth

¼ teaspoon salt

¼ teaspoon freshly ground black pepper

1¼ cups crème fraîche

1. Coat the inside of the crock of the slow cooker with the butter. Slice the white parts of the leeks and about an inch of the green parts into ½"-thick slices; rinse well and drain. Add to the slow cooker along with the onion, carrots, potatoes, and turnips. Pour the boiling water or broth over the vegetables. Cover and cook on low for 8 hours or until all the vegetables are tender.

2. Use an immersion blender to purée the soup. Taste for seasoning and add salt and pepper if desired. Stir in the crème fraîche; cover and cook on low for 15 minutes or until the soup is brought back to temperature.

Slow Cooker Suggestions

To make your own crème fraîche, add 1 cup of heavy cream, ⅓ cup sour cream, and 2 tablespoons plain yogurt (with active acidophilus cultures) to a sterilized glass container. Mix, cover with plastic wrap, and let sit for 8 hours at room temperature. Refrigerate until ready to use or for up to a week.

Beef-Vegetable Soup

7 large carrots

2 celery stalks, finely diced

1 large sweet onion, peeled and diced

8 ounces fresh mushrooms, cleaned and sliced

1 tablespoon extra-virgin olive oil

1 teaspoon butter, melted

1 clove garlic, peeled and minced

4 cups beef broth

6 medium potatoes, peeled and diced

1 tablespoon dried parsley

¼ teaspoon dried oregano

¼ teaspoon dried rosemary

1 bay leaf, dried

¼ teaspoon salt

¼ teaspoon freshly ground black pepper

1 (3-pound) chuck roast

1 (10-ounce) package frozen green beans, thawed

1 (10-ounce) package frozen whole kernel corn, thawed

1 (10-ounce) package frozen baby peas, thawed

Fresh parsley sprigs

1. Peel the carrots. Dice 6 of the carrots and grate 1. Add the grated carrot, celery, onion, mushrooms, oil, and butter to the slow cooker. Stir to coat the vegetables in the oil and butter. Cover and cook on high for 30 minutes or until the vegetables are soft.

2. Stir in the garlic. Add the broth, diced carrots, potatoes, dried parsley, oregano, rosemary, bay leaf, salt, and pepper. Trim the roast of any fat and cut into bite-sized pieces. Cover and cook on low for 6 hours or until the beef is tender and the potatoes are cooked through.

3. Remove and discard the bay leaf. Stir in the green beans, corn, and peas; cover and cook on low for 1 hour or until the vegetables are heated through. Taste for seasoning and add additional salt, pepper, and herbs if needed. Garnish with parsley.

Slow Cooker Suggestions

Make Beef-Vegetable Soup a tomato-based dish by substituting 2 (14.5-ounce) cans of diced tomatoes for the beef broth.

Pho

1 tablespoon coriander seeds

1 tablespoon whole cloves

6 star anise

1 cinnamon stick

1 tablespoon fennel seed

1 tablespoon whole cardamom

4" knob fresh gingerroot, sliced

1 medium onion, peeled and sliced

Water, as needed

3 pounds beef knuckles or oxtails

1 quart Beef Stock (see recipe in Chapter 2)

¾ pound thinly sliced lean beef

8 ounces Vietnamese rice noodles

½ cup chopped fresh cilantro leaves

½ cup chopped fresh Thai basil leaves

2 cups mung bean sprouts

1. Quickly heat the spices, ginger, and onion in a dry nonstick skillet until the seeds start to pop. The onion and ginger should look slightly caramelized. Place them in a cheesecloth packet and tie it securely.

2. Fill a large pot with water. Bring the water to a boil and add the beef knuckles. Boil for 10 minutes. Remove from the heat and skim off the foam that rises to the surface.

3. Place the bones and the cheesecloth packet into a 6–7-quart slow cooker. Add the stock and fill the slow cooker with water, leaving 1" of headroom. Cook on low for up to 10 hours or overnight. Strain off any solids. Remove the bones and the packet.

4. Add the sliced beef and noodles. Cook for about 15 minutes or until the beef is cooked and the noodles are tender.

5. Garnish each bowl with cilantro, basil, and sprouts.

Southwestern Cheese Soup

2 pounds lean ground beef

1 envelope taco seasoning mix

1 (15.25-ounce) can whole kernel corn

1 (15-ounce) can kidney beans

1 (14.5-ounce) can diced tomatoes

2 (14.5-ounce) cans stewed tomatoes

1 (7-ounce) can green chilies, drained and minced

2 pounds Velveeta cheese, cut into cubes

1. Fry the ground beef in a large nonstick skillet over medium-high heat, breaking it apart as you do so. Drain and discard any fat rendered from the beef.

2. Transfer the ground beef to the slow cooker and stir the taco seasoning mix into the meat. Add the corn, beans, diced tomatoes, stewed tomatoes, and chilies to the slow cooker. Cover and cook on low for 4 hours.

3. Stir the cheese into the soup. Cover and, stirring occasionally, continue to cook on low for 30 minutes or until the cheese is melted and blended into the soup.

Quick and Easy Stew

SERVES

1 (2-pound) chuck roast

1 (10.5-ounce) can condensed French onion soup

1 (10.75-ounce) can condensed tomato soup

4 cups water

1½ (1-pound) bags frozen soup vegetables, thawed

¼ teaspoon freshly ground black pepper

2 tablespoons red wine or balsamic vinegar (optional)

Trim the fat from the roast and cut into bite-sized pieces. Add to the slow cooker along with the soups and water; stir to mix. Add the vegetables and pepper. Cover and cook on low for 8 hours or until the beef is tender and the vegetables are cooked through. Stir in wine or vinegar (as a flavor enhancer) if desired.

Quick and Easy Stew, Too

SERVES

1 (2-pound) chuck roast

1 (10.75-ounce) can condensed cream of celery soup

1 (10.75-ounce) can condensed cream of mushroom soup

1 (10.5-ounce) can condensed French onion soup

2 cups water

1½ (1-pound) bags frozen soup vegetables, thawed

¼ teaspoon freshly ground black pepper

Trim the fat from the roast and cut into bite-sized pieces. Add to the slow cooker along with the soups and water; stir to mix. Add the vegetables and pepper. Cover and cook on low for 8 hours or until the beef is tender and the vegetables are cooked through.

Basic Beef Stew

4 tablespoons vegetable oil

⅓ cup brown rice flour

1 tablespoon garlic powder

1 teaspoon salt

1 teaspoon ground black pepper

2 pounds beef chuck, cubed

1 medium onion, peeled and diced

6 large potatoes, peeled and diced

6 medium carrots, peeled and sliced

3 celery stalks, sliced

4 cups gluten-free beef broth

1. Grease a 4–6-quart slow cooker with nonstick cooking spray. Heat the oil in a large skillet over medium-high heat.

2. In a zip-top plastic bag, mix together the flour, garlic powder, salt, and pepper. Add a small handful of beef and shake until well coated. Repeat until all beef is coated in the flour mixture.

3. In batches brown beef in the hot oil, about 1 minute per side. Remove the browned meat and place in the slow cooker.

4. Lower the heat under the skillet to medium and add the onions. Cook until softened, about 3–5 minutes, then place on top of the beef in the slow cooker.

5. Add the remaining ingredients to slow cooker. Cover and cook on high for 4 hours or on low for 6–8 hours.

Beef Stew

3 tablespoons cooking oil

2 pounds beef stew meat

15 fingerling potatoes, skins on

1½ cups peeled sliced onions

1 tablespoon ginger-garlic paste

1 teaspoon ground cayenne pepper

1½ teaspoons garam masala powder (available in the Indian food section of most grocery stores)

3 bay leaves, dried

1 teaspoon turmeric

½ teaspoon fennel seeds

½ cup curry paste (available in the Indian food section of most grocery stores)

¼ teaspoon salt

½ cup diced canned pineapple, with juice

1 (8-ounce) can tomato sauce

1½ tablespoons butter

½ cup chopped fresh cilantro leaves

1. Heat the oil in a skillet. Add the meat and cook it for 8–10 minutes, browning it on all sides. Drain excess fat and discard.
2. Layer the bottom of the slow cooker with potatoes and onion. Top it with the beef.
3. In a medium bowl, mix the ginger-garlic paste, all the spices, the curry paste, salt, pineapple, and tomato sauce and pour it over the meat. Add the butter. Cover and cook on low for 8–10 hours.
4. Garnish with cilantro and serve with your favorite roti or rice dish.

Cuban Beef Stew

1 (2-pound) beef chuck roast

1 large onion, peeled and diced

2 cloves garlic, peeled and minced

1 red bell pepper, seeded and diced

1 green bell pepper, seeded and diced

4 strips bacon, chopped

1 (7-ounce) can green chilies, drained and minced

½ teaspoon dried thyme

½ teaspoon ground allspice

¼ teaspoon freshly grated nutmeg

1 cup beef broth

1 cup tomato juice

¼ teaspoon salt

¾ teaspoon freshly ground black pepper

3 large sweet potatoes

1. Trim the beef of any fat and cut into 1" cubes. Add it to the slow cooker along with all of the other ingredients except for the sweet potatoes. Stir to mix.

2. Peel and cut the sweet potatoes in half; add to the top of the other ingredients. Cover and cook on low for 8 hours or until the beef is tender.

Slow Cooker Suggestions

You can either serve a half slow-cooked sweet potato with each serving of the Cuban Beef Stew or, if you've added the sweet potato halves as instructed, cut them into cubes after they've cooked and carefully stir them into the stew. If you want sweet potato cubes that remain firm enough to stir into the stew without the risk of them falling apart, peel and dice the sweet potatoes and wait to stir them into the stew until the final 2–3 hours of the cooking time.

Beef Stew with Root Vegetables and Raisins

SERVES 8

1 tablespoon vegetable oil

1 tablespoon butter, melted

1 large onion, peeled and diced

1 celery stalk, finely diced

2 tablespoons all-purpose flour

¼ teaspoon salt

¼ teaspoon freshly ground black pepper

1 (2-pound) beef chuck roast, cut into 1" cubes

1 (1-pound) bag baby carrots

2 large parsnips, peeled and diced

2 large Yukon Gold or red potatoes, peeled and diced

2 (14.5-ounce) cans diced tomatoes, undrained

2 cups beef broth

2 cloves garlic, peeled and minced

1 bay leaf, dried

1 teaspoon dried thyme, crushed

½ cup almond- or pimiento-stuffed green olives

⅓ cup golden raisins

1. Add the oil, butter, onion, and celery to the slow cooker. Cover and, stirring occasionally, cook on high for 30 minutes, or while you prepare the other ingredients.

2. Place the flour, salt, and pepper in a plastic bag and add the meat cubes; close and shake to coat the meat. Add half of the meat to the slow cooker, stirring it into the onion and celery.

3. Add the rest of the meat, the carrots, parsnips, potatoes, tomatoes, broth, garlic, bay leaf, and thyme to the cooker; stir to combine. Reduce the heat setting to low; cover and cook for 8 hours.

4. Remove and discard the bay leaf. Add the olives and raisins and stir. Serve warm.

Marsala Beef Stew

2 tablespoons extra-virgin olive oil

1 tablespoon butter or ghee

1 (2-pound) English-cut chuck roast, cut into bite-sized pieces

2 tablespoons all-purpose flour

1 small carrot, peeled and diced

1 celery stalk, finely diced

1 large yellow onion, peeled and diced

3 cloves garlic, peeled and minced

8 ounces mushrooms, cleaned and sliced

½ cup dry white wine

1 cup Marsala wine

½ teaspoon dried rosemary

½ teaspoon dried oregano

½ teaspoon dried basil

2 cups beef broth

2 cups water

¼ teaspoon salt

¼ teaspoon freshly ground black pepper

1. Add the oil and butter or ghee to a large nonstick skillet and bring it to temperature over medium-high heat.

2. Put the beef pieces and flour in a plastic food-safe bag; close and toss to coat the meat. Add as many pieces of beef that will fit in the pan without crowding and brown for 10 minutes or until all the meat takes on a dark outer color. Transfer the browned meat to the slow cooker.

3. Reduce the heat to medium and add the carrot and celery; sauté for 5 minutes or until soft. Add the onion and sauté until the onion is translucent. Add the garlic and sauté for an additional 30 seconds. Stir in the mushrooms; sauté until tender. Transfer the sautéed vegetables and mushrooms to the slow cooker.

4. Add the remaining flour-coated beef to the slow cooker; stir to mix.

5. Add the wines to the skillet, and stir to pick up any browned bits sticking to the pan. Pour into the slow cooker. Add the rosemary, oregano, basil, broth, water, salt, and pepper to the slow cooker. Cover and cook on low for 6–8 hours or until the meat is tender. (You may need to allow the stew to cook uncovered for an hour or so to evaporate any extra liquid.) The taste of the stew will benefit if you allow it to rest, uncovered, off of the heat for a half hour, and then put the crock back in the slow cooker over low heat long enough to bring it back to temperature, but that step isn't necessary; you can serve it immediately if you prefer.

Portuguese Beef Stew

SERVES 8

2 tablespoons extra-virgin olive oil

3 pounds beef bottom round

¼ teaspoon salt

¼ teaspoon freshly ground black pepper

1 large onion, peeled and diced

2 cloves garlic, peeled and minced

1 cup Zinfandel or other dry red wine

1 (6-ounce) can tomato paste

1 (28-ounce) can diced tomatoes

1 cup beef broth

1½ tablespoons pickling spices

1 bay leaf, dried

2 teaspoons dried mint

1. Add the oil to the slow cooker. Trim the beef of any fat and cut it into bite-sized pieces. Add the meat to the cooker along with the salt, pepper, onion, and garlic. Stir to coat the meat and vegetables in the oil.

2. Add the wine, tomato paste, undrained tomatoes, and broth to a bowl or measuring cup. Stir to mix. Pour into the slow cooker. Add the pickling spices and bay leaf. Cover and cook on low for 7 hours or until the beef is cooked through and tender. Skim and discard any fat from the surface of the stew in the slow cooker. Remove and discard the bay leaf.

3. Stir in the dried mint; cover and continue to cook on low for 15 minutes to allow the mint to blend into the stew. (If you have fresh mint available, you can instead sprinkle about 1 teaspoon of minced fresh mint leaves over each serving. Garnish each serving with a sprig of mint as well if desired.)

Slow Cooker Suggestions

When pickling spices are used in a dish, they're usually added to a muslin cooking bag or a tea ball or tied into a piece of cheesecloth. After the cooking time, they're pulled from the pot and discarded. For the Portuguese Beef Stew recipe, if you wish, you can simply stir them in with the other ingredients.

Beef and Sweet Potato Stew

¾ cup brown rice flour

1½ teaspoons salt, divided

1½ teaspoons ground black pepper, divided

1¼ pounds stew beef, cut into 1" chunks

¼ cup olive oil, divided

1 medium yellow onion, peeled and diced

2 cups peeled and diced carrots

¾ pound cremini mushrooms, cleaned and cut in half

6 cloves garlic, peeled and minced

3 tablespoons tomato paste

½ cup red wine

1 pound sweet potatoes, peeled and diced

4 cups beef broth

1 bay leaf, dried

1½ teaspoons dried thyme

1 tablespoon gluten-free Worcestershire sauce

1 tablespoon sugar

1. In a large zip-top plastic bag, place flour, 1 teaspoon salt, and 1 teaspoon pepper. Add beef and close the bag. Shake lightly and open the bag and make sure that all of the beef is coated in flour and seasoning. Set aside.

2. In a large skillet, heat 2 tablespoons of olive oil over medium heat. Cook the beef in small batches until browned on all sides, about 1 minute per side. Add the beef to a greased 4–6-quart slow cooker.

3. In the same skillet, heat the remaining 2 tablespoons of olive oil. Add the onion and carrots and cook until onions are translucent, about 5 minutes.

4. Add mushrooms and garlic and cook for another 2–3 minutes.

5. Add tomato paste and heat through. Deglaze the pan with the wine, scraping the stuck-on bits from the bottom of the pan. Add the cooked vegetable mixture on top of the beef in the slow cooker.

6. Add the sweet potatoes, broth, bay leaf, thyme, and Worcestershire sauce. Cover and cook on low for 8 hours or on high for 4 hours.

7. Before serving, add sugar and remaining salt and pepper.

Beef and Vegetable Stew

2 teaspoons canola oil

1 large onion, peeled and diced

2 medium parsnips, peeled and diced

2 medium carrots, peeled and diced

2 celery stalks, diced

3 cloves garlic, peeled and minced

2 medium red skin potatoes, scrubbed and diced

1 tablespoon minced fresh tarragon leaves

2 tablespoons minced fresh rosemary leaves

1 pound lean beef top round roast, cut into 1" cubes

¼ teaspoon salt

½ teaspoon freshly ground black pepper

1½ cups water

½ cup frozen peas

1 bulb fennel, diced

1 tablespoon minced fresh parsley leaves

1. Heat the oil in a large skillet. Sauté the onion, parsnips, carrots, celery, garlic, potatoes, tarragon, rosemary, and beef until the ingredients begin to soften and brown. Drain off any excess fat.

2. Place the mixture into a 4-quart slow cooker. Sprinkle with salt and pepper. Pour in the water. Stir. Cook for 8–9 hours on low.

3. Add the frozen peas and fennel. Cover and cook an additional ½ hour on high. Stir in the parsley before serving.

Beef and Guinness Stew

2 teaspoons olive oil

1 large onion, peeled and diced

2 medium parsnips, peeled and diced

2 medium carrots, peeled and diced

2 celery stalks, diced

3 cloves garlic, peeled and minced

2 large russet potatoes, peeled and diced

2 tablespoons minced fresh rosemary leaves

2 pounds lean beef top round roast, cut into 1" cubes

1 tablespoon honey

¼ teaspoon kosher salt

½ teaspoon freshly ground black pepper

1 tablespoon baking cocoa

1 cup water

½ cup Guinness Extra Stout

1. Spray a 4–5-quart slow cooker with nonstick olive oil cooking spray.

2. Heat the oil in a large skillet over medium-high heat. Sauté the onion, parsnips, carrots, celery, garlic, and potatoes until softened, about 10 minutes. Stir in rosemary and beef. Sauté until the beef is browned, about 5 minutes more. Drain any excess fat.

3. Add beef and vegetables to the slow cooker. Drizzle with honey and sprinkle with salt, pepper, and cocoa. Pour in the water and Guinness. Stir. Cook for 8–9 hours on low.

4. Stir before serving to fully mix the cooked ingredients together.

Slow Cooker Suggestions

Leaner cuts like top round are excellent choices for slow cooking because the long cooking time tenderizes them. Look for cuts that have minimal marbling and trim off any excess fat before cooking. Searing and sautéing are good ways to cook off some external fat before adding the meat to the slow cooker. Drain any excess fat.

Spanish Beef Stew

1 tablespoon olive oil

2 cloves garlic, peeled and sliced

1 medium onion, peeled and sliced

3 slices bacon, cut into 1" pieces

1 pound stew beef, cubed

3 large Roma tomatoes, diced

1 bay leaf, crumbled

¼ teaspoon dried sage

¼ teaspoon dried marjoram

½ teaspoon paprika

½ teaspoon curry powder

1 teaspoon kosher salt

2 tablespoons vinegar

1 cup Beef Stock (see recipe in Chapter 2)

½ cup white wine

4 medium potatoes, peeled and sliced

⅓ cup pitted, sliced olives

2 tablespoons chopped fresh parsley leaves

1. Spray a 4–5-quart slow cooker with nonstick olive oil cooking spray. Heat oil in a large skillet over medium heat. Sauté the garlic, onion, bacon, and beef until the bacon and beef are done and the onion softened. Drain and transfer the meat mixture to the slow cooker.

2. Add the tomatoes, bay leaf, sage, marjoram, paprika, curry powder, salt, vinegar, stock, and wine to the slow cooker. Cover and cook on low for 5 hours.

3. Add the potatoes, olives, and parsley to the slow cooker and cook for 1 hour more.

CHAPTER 4

Chicken

Chicken-Noodle Soup

4 bone-in chicken thighs, skin removed

2 bone-in chicken breasts, skin removed

4 large carrots, peeled and sliced

1 large sweet onion, peeled and diced

2 celery stalks, diced

1 teaspoon salt

2 teaspoons dried parsley

¾ teaspoon dried marjoram

½ teaspoon dried basil

¼ teaspoon poultry seasoning

¼ teaspoon freshly ground black pepper

1 bay leaf, dried

8 cups water

2½ cups medium egg noodles, uncooked

2 large eggs

1. Add the chicken thighs and breasts, carrots, onion, celery, salt, parsley, marjoram, basil, poultry seasoning, black pepper, bay leaf, and 6 cups of the water to the slow cooker. Cover and cook on low for 8 hours. Move the chicken to a cutting board. Remove and discard the bay leaf.

2. Increase the temperature of the slow cooker to high. Add the remaining 2 cups of water. Stir in the noodles and cook, covered, on high for 20 minutes or until the noodles are cooked through.

3. While the noodles cook, remove the meat from the bones. Cut the chicken into bite-sized pieces or shred it with 2 forks.

4. Ladle about ½ cup of the broth from the slow cooker into a bowl. Add the eggs and whisk to mix; stir the egg mixture into the slow cooker along with the chicken. Cover and cook for 15 minutes.

Matzo Ball Soup

2 quarts Chicken Stock (see recipe in Chapter 2)

1 celery stalk, diced

2 medium carrots, peeled and cut into coin-sized pieces

1 medium parsnip, peeled and diced

1 medium onion, peeled and diced

1½ cups diced cooked chicken

1 cup boiling water

1 cup matzo meal

1 egg

1½ tablespoons minced fresh dill

1. Put the Chicken Stock, celery, carrots, parsnip, and onions into a 4-quart slow cooker. Cook on low for 6–8 hours. Add the chicken 1 hour before serving.

2. About 20 minutes before serving, mix the boiling water, matzo meal, egg, and dill in a large bowl until smooth. Form into 2" balls. Drop them into the soup, cover, and cook for 15 minutes.

Slow Cooker Suggestions

Matzo meal, a product similar to bread crumbs, is made from crushed matzo. While it is available year-round, it is particularly easy to find near Passover. You can make matzo meal at home by pulsing matzo (flat unleavened crackers) in a food processor until small crumbs form. It is a necessary ingredient in matzo balls and can be used as a substitute for bread crumbs in many recipes.

Chicken Tortilla Soup

4 corn tortillas

½ teaspoon canola oil

1 teaspoon ground cumin

1 teaspoon chili powder

1 teaspoon smoked paprika

⅛ teaspoon salt

1 (28-ounce) can crushed tomatoes

1 (14.5-ounce) can fire-roasted diced tomatoes

3 cups Chicken Stock (see recipe in Chapter 2)

2 cloves garlic, peeled and minced

1 medium onion, peeled and diced

1 (4-ounce) can diced green chilies, drained

2 habanero peppers, seeded and diced

1 cup fresh corn kernels

2 cups cubed cooked chicken or turkey breast

1. Slice tortillas in half, then into ¼" strips. Heat canola oil in a shallow skillet. Add the tortilla strips and cook, turning once, until they are crisp and golden. Drain on paper towel–lined plates. Blot dry. Divide evenly among the bowls of soup before serving.

2. Place the spices, tomatoes, stock, garlic, onions, chilies, and peppers in a 4-quart slow cooker. Cover and cook on low for 6 hours.

3. After 6 hours, add the corn and turkey or chicken. Cover and cook for an additional 45–60 minutes.

Herbed Chicken and Vegetable Soup

7 large carrots

2 celery stalks, finely diced

1 large sweet onion, peeled and diced

8 ounces fresh mushrooms, cleaned and sliced

1 tablespoon extra-virgin olive oil

1 teaspoon butter, melted

1 clove garlic, peeled and minced

4 cups chicken broth

6 medium potatoes, peeled and diced

1 tablespoon dried parsley

¼ teaspoon dried oregano

¼ teaspoon dried rosemary

1 bay leaf, dried

2 strips orange zest

¼ teaspoon salt

¼ teaspoon freshly ground black pepper

8 chicken thighs, skin removed

1 (10-ounce) package frozen green beans, thawed

1 (10-ounce) package frozen whole kernel corn, thawed

1 (10-ounce) package frozen baby peas, thawed

Fresh parsley sprigs

1. Peel the carrots. Dice 6 of the carrots and grate 1. Add the grated carrot, celery, onion, mushrooms, oil, and butter to the slow cooker. Stir to coat the vegetables in the oil and butter. Cover and cook on high for 30 minutes or until the vegetables are soft.

2. Stir in the garlic. Add the broth, diced carrots, potatoes, dried parsley, oregano, rosemary, bay leaf, orange zest, salt, pepper, and chicken thighs. Cover and cook on low for 6 hours.

3. Use a slotted spoon to remove the thighs, cut the meat from the bone and into bite-sized pieces, and return it to the pot. Remove and discard the orange zest and bay leaf. Stir in the green beans, corn, and peas; cover and cook on low for 1 hour or until the vegetables are heated through. Taste for seasoning and add additional salt, pepper, and herbs if needed. Garnish with parsley.

Chicken Vegetable Soup

½ cup chopped onions

1 (14.5-ounce) can Italian-seasoned diced tomatoes

1 (14.5-ounce) can low-sodium mixed vegetables

1 (14.5-ounce) can low-sodium chicken broth

1 (10-ounce) can chunk chicken, drained

1. Spray a 4–5-quart slow cooker with nonstick olive oil cooking spray.
2. Place onions in a small glass or microwave-safe bowl. Cover with plastic wrap and cook on high for 1–2 minutes until onions are soft.
3. Add softened onions, tomatoes, mixed vegetables, and chicken broth to prepared slow cooker. Cook on high for 4 hours or on low for 8 hours.
4. Thirty minutes prior to serving add chicken to the slow cooker. Stir to warm through.

Caraway Soup

1 cube chicken bouillon

3 cups chicken broth

3 pounds cabbage, coarsely chopped

½ cup diagonally sliced celery

1 tablespoon kosher salt

½ tablespoon caraway seeds

¼ tablespoon ground black pepper

1 tablespoon tapioca

1 cup heavy cream

1. Spray a 4–5-quart slow cooker with nonstick olive oil cooking spray. Dissolve the bouillon cube in the broth and pour into the slow cooker.
2. Stir in the cabbage, celery, salt, caraway seeds, pepper, and tapioca. Cover and cook on low for 4½ hours.
3. Stir in the cream and cook for 30 minutes more.

Comforting Chicken and Rice Soup

1 tablespoon extra-virgin olive oil

1 medium onion, peeled and chopped

2 cloves garlic, peeled and minced

2 celery ribs, halved lengthwise and cut into ½"-thick slices

2 medium carrots, peeled and cut diagonally into ½"-thick slices

4 fresh thyme sprigs

1 bay leaf, dried

2 quarts (8 cups) gluten-free chicken broth

1 cup water

1 cup long-grain white rice

4 large boneless, skinless chicken breasts

1 teaspoon salt

1 teaspoon ground black pepper

1. In a large skillet heat olive oil. Add the onion, garlic, and celery. Cook and stir for about 6 minutes, until the vegetables are softened but not browned.
2. Add softened vegetables to a greased 6-quart slow cooker. Add remaining ingredients to the slow cooker.
3. Cover and cook on high for 4–6 hours or on low for 8–10 hours.
4. One hour prior to serving, use 2 forks to shred cooked chicken in the slow cooker and stir throughout the soup.

Aromatic Chicken Rice Soup

2 quarts Chicken Stock (see recipe in Chapter 2)

2 carrots, peeled and diced

2 celery stalks, diced

2" knob fresh gingerroot, minced

½" knob galangal root, minced

2 tablespoons lime juice

1 onion, peeled and minced

4 cloves garlic, peeled and minced

⅛ teaspoon salt

½ teaspoon freshly ground black pepper

½ cup minced fresh cilantro leaves

1½ cups cooked rice

2 cups diced cooked chicken

1. Place the Chicken Stock, carrots, celery, ginger, galangal root, lime juice, onion, garlic, salt, and pepper in a 4-quart slow cooker. Stir. Cook on low for 7–9 hours.

2. Stir in the cilantro, rice, and chicken. Cook on high for 15–30 minutes. Stir prior to serving.

Gumbo

SERVES 8

2 tablespoons butter

2 tablespoons flour

1 cubanelle pepper, seeded and diced

4 cloves garlic, peeled and diced

1 large onion, peeled and diced

2 large carrots, peeled and diced

2 celery stalks, diced

1 quart Chicken Stock (see recipe in Chapter 2)

2 tablespoons Cajun seasoning

4 chicken andouille sausages, sliced

1½ cups diced fresh tomatoes

2 cups diced okra

1. In a nonstick skillet, melt the butter. Add the flour and stir until the flour is golden brown. Add the pepper, garlic, onions, carrots, and celery. Sauté for 1 minute.

2. Add the mixture to a 4-quart slow cooker. Add the stock, seasoning, sausage, and tomatoes. Cook on low for 8–10 hours.

3. Add the okra for the last hour of cooking. Stir prior to serving.

Herbed Chicken and Pasta Soup

SERVES 4

1 tablespoon olive oil

2 pounds boneless, skinless chicken breast, pounded to 1" thickness

1 teaspoon kosher salt

1 teaspoon freshly ground black pepper

2 large red onions, peeled and diced

2 medium carrots, peeled and diced

2 celery stalks, diced

¼ bunch fresh flat-leaf parsley leaves, chopped

1 tablespoon chopped fresh dill, divided

10 cups Chicken Stock (see recipe in Chapter 2)

½ cup chopped fresh spinach

1 teaspoon fresh thyme leaves

2 teaspoons lemon juice

1 cup uncooked orzo

1. Heat the olive oil in a large skillet over medium heat until it shimmers, about 1 minute. Season both sides of the chicken with salt and pepper. Cook chicken on one side for 5 minutes, flip, and cook for an additional 3 minutes.

2. Place the chicken in a 4–5-quart slow cooker with the onions, carrots, celery, parsley, and half the dill. Stir in the broth.

3. Simmer for 7½ hours on low heat. Add spinach, thyme, lemon juice, orzo, and remaining dill.

4. Cook for an additional 15–20 minutes or until orzo is plump.

Slow Cooker Suggestions

Did you know that dill is chockablock with antioxidants? And it contains vitamins like niacin, folic acid, vitamin A, and vitamin C. So keep fresh dill on hand for soups, stews, sauces, and even just as a snack with cucumber and a little vinegar. You can't go wrong with dill!

Chicken, Mushroom, and Barley Soup

SERVES

8

1 ounce dried porcini mushrooms

1 cup boiling water

2 tablespoons olive oil

2 medium carrots, peeled and diced

3 celery stalks, diced

1 large onion, peeled and diced

1 clove garlic, peeled and minced

6 cups Chicken Stock (see recipe in Chapter 2), divided

⅔ cup medium pearl barley

¼ teaspoon ground black pepper

2 cups cooked shredded chicken

1. Place the dried mushrooms in a medium heat-safe bowl. Pour the boiling water over the mushrooms. Soak for 15 minutes.

2. Heat olive oil in a large skillet set over medium-high heat. Sauté the carrots, celery, and onion together until the vegetables have softened and have some color, about 7–10 minutes. Drain mushrooms and add to vegetables in the skillet. Sauté for 5 minutes. Add garlic and sauté for 2 minutes. Transfer mixture to a 4–5-quart slow cooker.

3. Using 1 cup of the Chicken Stock, deglaze the pan, making sure to scoop up all the browned bits. Pour deglazed broth over vegetables along with the remaining 5 cups of stock.

4. Add barley and pepper and stir well. Cook 6 hours on low heat. Add cooked chicken and cook for another 30 minutes or until chicken is heated through.

Greek Lemon-Chicken Soup

4 cups gluten-free chicken broth

¼ cup fresh lemon juice

¼ cup shredded carrots

¼ cup chopped onion

¼ cup chopped celery

⅛ teaspoon ground white pepper

2 tablespoons butter

2 tablespoons brown rice flour

4 egg yolks

½ cup cooked white rice

½ cup diced, cooked boneless chicken breast

8 slices lemon

1. In a greased 4-quart slow cooker combine the chicken broth, lemon juice, carrots, onion, celery, and pepper. Cover and cook on high for 3–4 hours or on low for 6–8 hours.

2. One hour before serving, blend the butter and the flour together in a medium bowl with a fork. Remove 1 cup of hot broth from the slow cooker and whisk with the butter and flour. Add mixture back to the slow cooker.

3. In a small bowl, beat the egg yolks until light in color. Gradually add some of the hot soup to the egg yolks, stirring constantly. Return the egg mixture to the slow cooker.

4. Add the rice and cooked chicken. Cook on low for an additional hour. Ladle hot soup into bowls and garnish with lemon slices.

Brunswick Stew

2 slices bacon, diced

3 small onions, peeled and thinly sliced

1 red bell pepper, seeded and diced

3 tablespoons all-purpose flour

1 teaspoon salt

½ teaspoon ground black pepper

Pinch ground cayenne pepper

1 pound boneless, skinless chicken breast

1 pound boneless, skinless chicken thighs

1½ cups chicken broth

2 (14.5-ounce) cans diced tomatoes

½ teaspoon dried thyme, crushed

2 teaspoons dried parsley

1 tablespoon Worcestershire sauce

2 cups frozen lima beans, thawed

2 cups frozen whole kernel corn, thawed

½ cup frozen sliced okra, thawed

1. Add the bacon, onion, and red bell pepper to the slow cooker; cover and cook on high for 30 minutes.
2. Put the flour, salt, pepper, and cayenne in a gallon-sized food storage bag. Cut the chicken into bite-sized pieces, add to the bag, close the bag, and shake to coat the pieces with the seasoned flour.
3. Add the floured pieces to the slow cooker and stir them into the bacon, onions, and red bell pepper mixture.
4. Stir in the broth, tomatoes, thyme, parsley, and Worcestershire sauce. Cover and cook on low for 6–8 hours.
5. Add the lima beans, corn, and okra; cover and cook on low for 1 hour or until the vegetables are heated through.

Rosemary-Thyme Stew

SERVES 4

1 teaspoon canola oil

1 large onion, peeled and diced

1 tablespoon flour

1 large carrot, peeled and diced

2 celery stalks, diced

2 cloves garlic, peeled and minced

1 cup peeled and diced Yukon Gold potatoes

3½ tablespoons minced fresh thyme leaves

3 tablespoons minced fresh rosemary leaves

1 pound boneless, skinless chicken breast, cut into 1" cubes

¼ teaspoon salt

½ teaspoon freshly ground black pepper

1½ cups water or Chicken Stock (see recipe in Chapter 2)

½ cup frozen or fresh corn kernels

1. Heat the oil in a large skillet. Sauté the onion, flour, carrots, celery, garlic, potatoes, thyme, rosemary, and chicken until the chicken is white on all sides. Drain off any excess fat.

2. Put the sautéed ingredients into a 4-quart slow cooker. Sprinkle with salt and pepper. Pour in the water or stock. Stir. Cook for 8–9 hours on low.

3. Add the corn. Cover and cook an additional ½ hour on high. Stir before serving.

Tuscan Chicken and Sausage Stew

SERVES 4

1 pound boneless, skinless chicken thighs, cut into bite-sized pieces

8 ounces turkey sausage, cut into ½" slices

1 (24-ounce) jar pasta sauce

1 (14.5-ounce) can green beans, drained

1 teaspoon dried oregano

Place all ingredients in a greased 4–5-quart slow cooker. Stir to combine and cook on high for 4 hours or on low for 8 hours.

Creamy Chicken Stew

2 tablespoons olive oil

3 pounds boneless, skinless chicken breast, cut into 1" cubes

1 teaspoon salt

1 teaspoon ground black pepper

1 teaspoon paprika

2 cups peeled and cubed white potatoes

3 large carrots, peeled and diced

2 cups frozen whole kernel corn

1 cup seeded and chopped green pepper

1 cup seeded and chopped sweet red pepper

1 cup diced celery

1 medium onion, peeled and diced

2 teaspoons dried basil

1 bay leaf, dried

¼ teaspoon celery salt

7 cups gluten-free chicken broth

½ cup butter

⅓ cup brown rice flour

1. In a large skillet, heat the olive oil. Sauté chicken pieces in small batches until they are browned, about 1–2 minutes per side. Add the browned chicken to a greased 6-quart slow cooker.

2. Add the salt, pepper, paprika, potatoes, carrots, corn, green and red peppers, celery, onion, basil, bay leaf, celery salt, and chicken broth to the slow cooker. Cover and cook on high for 4 hours or on low for 8 hours. One hour before serving remove the bay leaf.

3. In a large saucepan, melt the butter; whisk in the flour until smooth. Cook and stir for 2 minutes. Gradually whisk in 2 cups of hot broth from the slow cooker. Bring to a boil; cook and stir for 2 minutes or until thickened. Whisk thickened sauce into the stew in the slow cooker. Cook an additional hour.

Spicy Chicken Stew

3 tablespoons cooking oil

3 teaspoons coarsely crushed black peppercorns

2 cinnamon sticks

5 green whole cardamom pods

7 whole cloves

1½ pounds boneless, skinless chicken pieces

1 tablespoon coriander powder

1½ teaspoons garam masala powder (available in the Indian food section of most grocery stores)

1 teaspoon turmeric

¼ teaspoon salt

1 cup peeled and thinly sliced onion

1 (14.5-ounce) can diced tomatoes, drained

1 (14-ounce) can chicken broth, or water

1½ tablespoons ginger-garlic paste

3 cups baby spinach

1. Heat the oil in a pan. Add the whole spices. As they sizzle, add the chicken. Stir-fry for 3–4 minutes. Drain the extra liquid. Transfer the chicken and whole spices to the slow cooker.

2. Add the remaining ingredients to the slow cooker *except* for the spinach. Stir. Cover and cook on high for 4–5 hours or on low for 8–9 hours.

3. Add the spinach. Stir everything together well. Turn off the heat. Cover and let it sit for 5–10 minutes. Remove whole spices. Serve hot with your favorite bread or rice dish. If the stew has more liquid than you prefer, transfer it to a pan (before adding the spinach) and cook on the stovetop on high for 5 minutes before serving.

Slow Cooker Suggestions

Slow-cooked chicken thighs stay juicier than breast pieces. Adding a teaspoon of papaya powder or a couple tablespoons of pineapple juice also helps.

Chicken and Mushroom Stew

SERVES 6

24 ounces boneless chicken, cut into 1" cubes, browned (in olive oil)

8 ounces fresh mushrooms, sliced

1 medium onion, peeled and diced

3 cups diced zucchini

1 cup seeded and diced green bell pepper

4 cloves garlic, peeled and minced

1 tablespoon olive oil

3 medium tomatoes, diced

1 (6-ounce) can tomato paste

¾ cup water

1 teaspoon each: dried thyme, oregano, marjoram, and basil

1. Add browned chicken to a 4–6-quart slow cooker.
2. In a sauté pan over medium heat, sauté the mushrooms, onion, zucchini, green pepper, and garlic in olive oil for 5–10 minutes, until crisp-tender, and add to the slow cooker.
3. Add the tomatoes, tomato paste, water, and seasonings.
4. Cover and cook on low for 4 hours or until the vegetables are tender. Serve hot.

Chicken Stew with Meat Sauce

1 pound 90% lean grass-fed ground beef

4 boneless, skinless chicken breasts

1 (6-ounce) can organic tomato paste

1 (28-ounce) can diced organic tomatoes, no salt added

4 cloves garlic, peeled and chopped

4 large carrots, peeled and sliced

2 red bell peppers, seeded and diced

2 green bell peppers, seeded and diced

1 tablespoon dried thyme

2 tablespoons olive oil

1 tablespoon chili powder

1. In a medium sauté pan, cook ground beef until browned, about 5 minutes. Drain and place in a 4–6-quart slow cooker.
2. Wipe out the sauté pan and place it over medium-high heat. Brown the chicken breasts (5 minutes per side). Add to the slow cooker.
3. Combine all the remaining ingredients in the slow cooker. Cook on high for 5 hours.
4. Serve over your favorite steamed vegetable.

CHAPTER 5

Pork and Lamb

Southwestern Soup

SERVES 4

1 pound pork tenderloin, cut into 1" pieces

1 cup chopped onion

1 green bell pepper, seeded and chopped

1 jalapeño pepper, seeded and minced

2 cloves garlic, peeled and minced

1 teaspoon chili powder

1 teaspoon ground cumin

¼ teaspoon freshly ground black pepper

5 cups Chicken Stock (see recipe in Chapter 2)

1 (14.5-ounce) can diced tomatoes

1 cup diced fresh avocado, for garnish

2 tablespoons chopped fresh cilantro leaves, for garnish

1. In the bottom of a 6-quart slow cooker, combine the pork, onion, bell pepper, jalapeño pepper, garlic, chili powder, cumin, and black pepper. Stir to combine.

2. Add stock and tomatoes. Cover and cook on low for 6–8 hours or on high for 3–4 hours.

3. When ready to serve, ladle into bowls and top with avocado and cilantro.

Ham, Cabbage, and Carrot Stew

SERVES 8

1 (2–3-pound) meaty ham bone

4 large carrots, peeled and sliced into 1" circles

½ head red or green cabbage, chopped

1 onion, peeled and chopped

8 cups gluten-free chicken broth

2 teaspoons salt

2 teaspoons ground black pepper

2 cups cooked cubed ham

1. Add ham bone, carrots, cabbage, onion, chicken broth, salt, and pepper to a greased 4–6-quart slow cooker. Cover and cook on high for 4–6 hours or on low for 8–10 hours.

2. One hour before serving remove the ham bone and add in the cubed ham pieces. Cook for an additional hour and serve.

Pork and Apple Stew

1 (3-pound) boneless pork shoulder roast

¼ teaspoon salt

¼ teaspoon freshly ground black pepper

1 large sweet onion, peeled and diced

2 Golden Delicious apples, peeled, cored, and diced

1 (2-pound) bag baby carrots

2 celery stalks, finely diced

2 cups apple juice or cider

¼ cup dry vermouth

2 tablespoons brandy

2 tablespoons brown sugar

½ teaspoon dried thyme

¼ teaspoon ground allspice

¼ teaspoon dried sage

2 large sweet potatoes, peeled and quartered

Trim the roast of any fat; discard the fat and cut the roast into bite-sized pieces. Add the pork to the slow cooker along with the remaining ingredients in the order given. (You want to rest the sweet potato quarters on top of the mixture in the slow cooker.) Cover and cook on low for 6 hours or until the pork is cooked through and tender.

Slow Cooker Suggestions

If you're unsure about the herbs and spices suggested in a recipe, wait to add them until the end of the cooking time. Once the meat is cooked through, spoon out ¼ cup or so of the pan juices into a microwave-safe bowl. Add a pinch of each herb and spice (in proportion to how they're suggested in the recipe), microwave on high for 15–30 seconds, and then taste the broth to see if you like it. Season the dish accordingly.

Slow Cooker Pork Posole

SERVES 8

2 pounds lean cubed pork

2 (15-ounce) cans white or yellow hominy, drained and rinsed

1 (28-ounce) can cubed potatoes, drained and rinsed

2 (14.5-ounce) cans diced tomatoes with green chilies, undrained

2 cups warm water

1 cup chopped carrots

4 cloves garlic, peeled and minced

1 medium onion, peeled and chopped

2 teaspoons ground cumin

2 teaspoons chili powder

1 teaspoon red pepper flakes

1 teaspoon dried oregano

1. Add all ingredients to a greased 4-quart slow cooker. Cook on low for 8 hours or on high for 4 hours.

2. Serve with shredded cheese, diced avocados, sliced black olives, pico de gallo, pickled jalapeño peppers, or sour cream, if desired.

Slow Cooker Suggestions

Hominy is corn that has been soaked in a weak lye solution. This treatment gives the corn a creamy white texture and a distinctive taste, as it removes the germ and the bran of the grain. Hominy that has been roughly ground is known as hominy grits and is often served for breakfast.

Filipino-Influenced Pork Chili

1 pound pork loin, cubed

1½ cups crushed tomatoes

⅓ cup banana sauce

2 tablespoons lime juice

2 tablespoons cane vinegar

1 teaspoon ginger juice

1 teaspoon chili powder

½ teaspoon freshly ground black pepper

2 jarred pimentos, minced

1 medium onion, peeled and minced

3 unripe plantains, peeled and diced

2 medium tomatoes, cubed

1 large sweet potato, scrubbed and cubed

1. Sauté the cubed pork in a dry skillet for 5 minutes. Drain off any fat.
2. Add the pork and remaining ingredients to a 4-quart slow cooker. Stir. Cook on low for 8 hours. Stir before serving.

Slow Cooker Suggestions

Banana sauce, also know as banana ketchup, is a popular condiment in the Philippines. Despite its similar appearance to tomato ketchup, it contains a mixture of bananas, sugar, vinegar, and spices rather than tomatoes. Banana sauce is found in Filipino-style spaghetti sauce and used on hot dogs, burgers, omelets, French fries, and fish.

Smoky Chipotle Pork Chili

1 pound ground pork

2 (14.5-ounce) canned fire-roasted diced tomatoes

3 chipotle chilies in adobo, chopped

1 teaspoon liquid smoke

1 teaspoon chili powder

1 teaspoon ground chipotle powder

1 teaspoon hot paprika

1 teaspoon smoked paprika

2 (15.5-ounce) cans chili beans, drained and rinsed

1 medium onion, peeled and diced

3 cloves garlic, peeled and minced

1. Quickly sauté the pork in a nonstick skillet until just cooked through. Drain off any fat.

2. Place all ingredients in a 4-quart slow cooker. Stir. Cook on low for 8–10 hours.

Lamb Stew

1½ pounds boneless lamb shoulder, fat trimmed

1 cup Beef Stock (see recipe in Chapter 2)

6 medium carrots, peeled and cut into ¾" pieces

12 ounces turnips, peeled and cut into ¾" pieces

¾ cup chopped onions

½ tablespoon crushed garlic

¼ teaspoon dried thyme

¼ teaspoon dried rosemary, crumbled

½ teaspoon ground black pepper

1. Cut lamb into 1½" chunks.

2. Combine all the ingredients into a 4-quart slow cooker and cook on low for 8–10 hours.

3. Before serving, skim off and discard fat.

Irish Coddle

6 strips bacon

1½ pounds pork sausage

¼ teaspoon salt

¼ teaspoon freshly ground black pepper

1 large yellow onion, peeled and diced

3 large potatoes, peeled and diced

3 large carrots, peeled and diced

1 cup beer, chicken broth, hard cider, or water

1. Cut the bacon into 1" pieces and add to a large nonstick skillet along with the sausage. Cook the bacon and brown the sausage over medium-high heat for about 10 minutes, breaking apart the sausage as you do so. Add salt, pepper, and the onion; sauté the onion for 5 minutes or until it is translucent. Drain the meat and onion mixture of any excess fat; discard the fat.

2. Spread ⅓ of the meat-onion mixture over the bottom of a slow cooker. Add the potatoes in a layer, sprinkling them with salt and pepper if desired. Spoon another ⅓ of the meat-onion mixture over the potatoes. Top that with the carrots in a layer. Spread the remaining meat-onion mixture over the top of the carrots.

3. Pour in the beer, broth, hard cider, or water. Cover and cook on low for 6 hours or until the vegetables are tender. Stir to mix; taste for seasoning and adjust if necessary. Ladle into bowls to serve.

Green Chili Stew

1 stick butter, melted

¼ cup all-purpose flour

4 cups chicken broth

1 large yellow onion, peeled and diced

½ teaspoon dried oregano

½ tablespoon granulated garlic

1 tablespoon chili powder

1 (28-ounce) can heat-and-serve pork

3 (7-ounce) cans mild or hot green chilies, drained and chopped

¼ teaspoon salt

¼ teaspoon freshly ground black pepper

Sour cream (optional)

1. Add the butter to the slow cooker and whisk in the flour, and then gradually whisk in the broth.
2. Stir in the onion, oregano, garlic, chili powder, pork, and canned chilies. Cover and cook on low for 6 hours. Stir well and taste for seasoning; add salt and pepper if needed. Add a dollop of sour cream over each serving if desired.

Slow Cooker Suggestions

For the Green Chili Stew, you can substitute chicken for the pork, or use slow-cooked, pulled pork shoulder roast and part of its broth instead of the canned pork and some of the chicken broth.

Bacon Corn Chowder

4 slices bacon, diced

1 medium red onion, peeled and chopped

½ jalapeño pepper, seeded and finely chopped

1 clove garlic, peeled and minced

2 tablespoons brown rice flour

½ teaspoon salt

¼ teaspoon ground black pepper

2 (15-ounce) cans sweet corn kernels, drained, or 4 cups frozen sweet corn

3 red potatoes (about 1 pound), peeled and diced

4 cups gluten-free chicken broth

2 cups half-and-half

1 cup chopped cherry tomatoes

3 tablespoons sliced fresh basil leaves

1. In a large pan, sauté the bacon until crispy and browned. Remove the bacon and set aside. Sauté the onion in the bacon grease until translucent, about 3–5 minutes.

2. Whisk in the jalapeño, garlic, flour, salt, and pepper and cook for 1 minute more until the flour is toasted.

3. Grease a 4–6-quart slow cooker with nonstick cooking spray. Add the onion mixture to the slow cooker. Add the corn, potatoes, and chicken broth. Stir the ingredients together.

4. Cover and cook on high for 4 hours or on low for 8 hours.

5. One hour before serving stir in the half-and-half. Add additional salt and pepper if desired. Serve the chowder by ladling into large bowls and garnishing with bacon, chopped tomatoes, and fresh basil.

Thick and Hearty Lancashire Lamb Stew

¼ cup olive oil

½ cup all-purpose flour

1 teaspoon kosher salt

½ teaspoon ground black pepper

2 pounds lamb stew meat

2 slices bacon, chopped

4 cloves garlic, peeled and chopped

2 large onions, peeled and chopped

2 large carrots, peeled and chopped

2 bay leaves, dried

2 cups Chicken Stock (see recipe in Chapter 2)

1 cup dry white wine

½ bunch fresh parsley sprigs

2 tablespoons dried rosemary

Juice and zest of ½ lemon

2 teaspoons Worcestershire sauce

1 (1-pound) bag great northern beans, soaked overnight and then simmered for 5 hours, or 2½ (15-ounce) cans white beans, drained

1. Heat the olive oil in a large skillet over medium-high heat.
2. In a shallow bowl, combine the flour, salt, and pepper. Dredge the lamb in the flour mixture. Brown the meat in the hot oil, about 1 minute on each side. Remove from the pan and drain.
3. In the same pan, cook the bacon until crisp. Place the lamb and bacon in a 6-quart slow cooker. Add the remaining ingredients to the slow cooker.
4. Cover and cook on high for 4 hours or on low for 8 hours.

Kerala Mutton Stew

2 tablespoons cooking oil

1½ pounds mutton

1 (14-ounce) can coconut milk

¾ cup caramelized onions

1 tablespoon thinly sliced fresh gingerroot

4 green chilies, seeded and thinly sliced

1 cup cubed and peeled yellow potatoes

1 cup baby carrots

¾ cup frozen corn, thawed

¼ teaspoon salt

1 tablespoon coconut oil

¼ teaspoon whole cloves

1 cinnamon stick

½ teaspoon turmeric

18 curry leaves (available at Asian markets)

1 teaspoon ground cayenne pepper

1. On the stovetop, heat the cooking oil in a skillet over medium heat. Add the mutton and brown it. Set aside.
2. Open the can of coconut milk. Skim out all the cream on top and put in a separate bowl, leaving just the diluted water in the bottom. Set aside.
3. In the slow cooker, add the caramelized onions, ginger, green chilies, meat, and vegetables. Add the salt and reserved coconut water. Cover and cook for 4 hours on high setting or on low for about 8–9 hours.
4. In a tempering pan, heat the coconut oil. Add the cloves, cinnamon stick, turmeric, and curry leaves. As they splutter, turn off the heat. Set aside.
5. Uncover the slow cooker. Add the skimmed coconut cream, cayenne pepper, and tempered oil and spices. Stir well. Cover and cook for another hour on high or until the meat is well cooked. Serve hot with steamed rice or *appam* (fermented rice pancake).

CHAPTER 6

Seafood

Étouffée

2 tablespoons vegetable oil

1 large onion, peeled and diced

6 green onions

2 celery stalks, finely diced

1 green bell pepper, seeded and diced

1 jalapeño pepper, seeded and diced

2 cloves garlic, peeled and minced

3 tablespoons tomato paste

3 (14.5-ounce) cans diced tomatoes

¼ teaspoon salt

½ teaspoon dried basil

½ teaspoon dried oregano

½ teaspoon dried thyme

¼ teaspoon ground cayenne pepper

1 pound raw shrimp, peeled and deveined

1 pound scallops, quartered

2 teaspoons cornstarch

1 tablespoon cold water

Hot sauce, to taste

1. Add the oil and onion to the slow cooker. Clean the green onions and chop the white parts and about 1" of the greens. Add to the slow cooker along with the celery, green bell pepper, and jalapeño. Stir to coat the vegetables in the oil. Cover and cook on high for 30 minutes or until the vegetables are soft.

2. Stir in the garlic and tomato paste. Cover and cook on high for 15 minutes.

3. Stir in the tomatoes, salt, basil, oregano, thyme, and cayenne pepper. Reduce the heat setting of the slow cooker to low; cover and cook for 6 hours.

4. Stir in the shrimp and scallops. Increase the heat setting of the slow cooker to high, cover, and cook for 15 minutes.

5. Add the cornstarch and water to a small bowl. Stir to mix. Remove any lumps if necessary. Uncover the slow cooker and stir in the cornstarch mixture. Cook and stir for 5 minutes, or until the mixture is thickened and the cornstarch flavor is cooked out. Stir in hot sauce, to taste.

Skinny Slow Cooker Chowder

SERVES 4

1 large onion, peeled and chopped

2 cloves garlic, peeled and finely chopped

2 medium red potatoes, peeled and diced

2 cups peeled and sliced carrots

4 celery stalks, chopped

2 (14.5-ounce) cans chicken broth

1 teaspoon sea salt

1 (1-pound) package frozen seafood mix, thawed

1 (12-ounce) can fat-free evaporated milk

3 tablespoons fresh Italian parsley leaves, chopped

1. Place onion, garlic, potatoes, carrots, celery, chicken broth, and salt in a 4–5-quart slow cooker. Cover and cook on high for 4–6 hours.

2. Stir thawed seafood mix and evaporated milk into the slow cooker. Cover and cook for 1 hour. Garnish with parsley and serve.

Hatteras Clam Chowder

SERVES 4

4 slices bacon, diced

1 small onion, peeled and diced

2 medium russet potatoes, peeled and diced

1 (8-ounce) bottle clam stock

3 cups water

½ teaspoon salt

½ teaspoon freshly ground black pepper

2 (6.5-ounce) cans minced clams (do not drain)

1. In a 2-quart or larger saucepan, sauté bacon until crispy and browned. Add onion and sauté until translucent, about 3–5 minutes. Add cooked onions and bacon to a greased 2.5-quart slow cooker.

2. Add potatoes, clam stock, and enough water to cover (2–3 cups). Add salt and pepper.

3. Cover and cook on high for 3 hours until potatoes are very tender.

4. One hour prior to serving add in the clams along with broth from the cans and cook until heated through.

Manhattan Scallop Chowder

2 tablespoons butter, melted

2 celery stalks, finely diced

1 medium green bell pepper, seeded and diced

1 large carrot, peeled and finely diced

1 medium onion, peeled and diced

2 large potatoes, scrubbed and diced

1 (14.5-ounce) can diced tomatoes

1 (15-ounce) can tomato purée

2 cups (bottled) clam juice

1 cup dry white wine

¾ cup water

1 teaspoon dried thyme

1 teaspoon dried parsley

1 bay leaf, dried

¼ teaspoon freshly ground black pepper

1½ pounds bay scallops

¼ teaspoon salt

Fresh parsley leaves, minced, enough for garnish

Fresh basil leaves for garnish

1. Add the butter, celery, bell pepper, and carrot to a slow cooker; stir to coat the vegetables in the butter. Cover and cook on high for 15 minutes. Stir in the onion. Cover and cook on high for 30 minutes or until the vegetables are soft.

2. Stir in the potatoes, tomatoes, tomato purée, clam juice, wine, water, thyme, dried parsley, bay leaf, and pepper. Cover, reduce the temperature to low, and cook for 7 hours or until the potatoes are cooked through.

3. Cut the scallops so that they are each no larger than 1" pieces. Add to the slow cooker, increase the temperature to high, cover, and cook for 15 minutes or until the scallops are firm. Remove and discard the bay leaf. Taste for seasoning and add salt or adjust other seasoning if necessary. Ladle into soup bowls. Sprinkle minced fresh parsley over each serving and garnish with fresh basil.

New England Corn Chowder

SERVES

½ cup Earth Balance Original Buttery Spread

1 onion, peeled and diced

3 cloves garlic, peeled and minced

¼ cup flour

4 cups unsweetened soy milk

3 medium potatoes, peeled and diced

2 cups frozen corn

2 cups Vegetable Stock (see recipe in Chapter 2)

½ teaspoon dried thyme

½ teaspoon salt

1. Add the Earth Balance to a 4-quart slow cooker and sauté the onion on high heat for 4–5 minutes. Add the garlic and sauté for 1 minute more.

2. Slowly stir in the flour with a whisk and create a roux. Stir in the soy milk and continue whisking until very smooth.

3. Add the remaining ingredients and cook on low heat for 3–4 hours.

Herbed Tilapia Stew

SERVES

2 pounds frozen boneless tilapia fillets

2 tablespoons butter

2 tablespoons olive oil

1 (14.5-ounce) can diced tomatoes, with juice

4 cloves garlic, peeled and minced

½ cup sliced green onions

2 teaspoons Worcestershire sauce

2 tablespoons fresh thyme leaves, chopped, or 1 teaspoon dried thyme

1. Grease a 4–5-quart slow cooker with nonstick cooking spray. Place all ingredients in the slow cooker.

2. Cover and cook on high for 1½–2 hours or on low for 2½–3 hours. Watch the cooking time. If the fish fillets are very thin you may need to reduce the cooking time.

3. When the fish is cooked through, fillets will easily separate and flake with a fork. Break the fish up into the tomatoes and cooking liquids.

Seafood Stew

2 tablespoons extra-virgin olive oil, plus more for serving

2 medium onions, peeled and diced

4 cloves garlic, peeled and minced

1 pound smoked sausage, sliced

½ teaspoon dried thyme

¼ teaspoon dried oregano, crushed

1 bay leaf, dried

8 large Yukon Gold potatoes, peeled and diced

8 cups chicken broth

1 pound kale, chopped

2 pounds perch, cod, or bass fillets, skin and pin bones removed

Hot water

2 (28-ounce) cans boiled baby clams, drained

¼ teaspoon sea salt

¼ teaspoon freshly ground black pepper

¼ cup fresh flat-leaf parsley leaves, minced

1. Add the oil, onions, garlic, and sausage to a slow cooker; stir to coat the onions in the oil. Cover and, stirring occasionally, cook on high for 30 minutes or until the onions are translucent.

2. Add the thyme, oregano, bay leaf, and potatoes, stirring everything to mix the herbs and coat the potatoes in the oil.

3. Pour in the chicken broth. Cover and cook on low for 4 hours.

4. Stir in the kale and fish. Add enough hot water to cover the fish if needed. Cover and continue to cook on low for 15 minutes.

5. Add the drained clams and cook on low for an additional 15 minutes or until the fish is cooked and the clams are brought to temperature. Taste for seasoning and add salt and pepper if needed. Garnish with chopped parsley and drizzle with extra-virgin olive oil.

Bouillabaisse

2 tablespoons extra-virgin olive oil

1 large yellow onion, peeled and sliced

4 green onions, cleaned and sliced

1 clove garlic, peeled and minced

2 cups tomato juice or chicken broth

1 (14.5-ounce) can diced tomatoes

1 cup Chardonnay or other dry white wine

2 cups water or Fish Stock (see recipe in Chapter 2)

1 bay leaf, dried

½ teaspoon freshly ground black pepper

1 teaspoon dried tarragon, crumbled

½ teaspoon dried thyme, crushed

1 tablespoon dried parsley, crushed

1 pound whitefish (halibut, cod, snapper), cut into 1" pieces

1 pound frozen cooked shrimp, thawed

2 (3.53-ounce) pouches whole baby clams

10 ounces boiled mussels, drained

1. Add the oil and onions to a slow cooker; cover and, stirring occasionally, cook on high for 30 minutes or until the onion slices are translucent.
2. Stir in the garlic, tomato juice or broth, tomatoes, wine, water or Fish Stock, bay leaf, pepper, tarragon, thyme, and parsley. Cover, reduce the slow cooker heat to low, and cook for 4–8 hours.
3. Gently stir in the fish pieces; cover and cook on low for 15 minutes. Stir in the shrimp, clams, and mussels; cover and cook on low for 15 minutes or until the fish is opaque and cooked through and all ingredients are brought to temperature.

Cioppino

1 medium onion, peeled and chopped

2 celery stalks, diced

6 cloves garlic, peeled and minced

1 (28-ounce) can diced tomatoes

8 ounces clam juice

¾ cup water or Fish Stock (see recipe in Chapter 2)

1 (6-ounce) can tomato paste

1 teaspoon red pepper flakes

2 tablespoons minced fresh oregano leaves

2 tablespoons minced fresh Italian parsley leaves

1 teaspoon red wine vinegar

10 ounces catfish nuggets

10 ounces peeled raw shrimp

6 ounces diced cooked clams

6 ounces lump crabmeat

¾ cup diced lobster meat

¼ cup diced green onion

1. Place the onions, celery, garlic, tomatoes, clam juice, water or stock, tomato paste, red pepper flakes, oregano, parsley, and vinegar in a 4-quart slow cooker. Stir vigorously. Cook on low for 8 hours.

2. Add the seafood and green onions and cook on high for 30 minutes. Stir prior to serving.

Slow Cooker Suggestions

Save your shrimp shells to make shrimp stock. Follow the recipe for Chicken Stock (see recipe in Chapter 2) and use the shells instead of chicken bones. Add a couple of extra pieces of celery, onion, and carrot for extra flavor. Use in seafood dishes instead of fish or chicken stock.

Aromatic Paella

3 tablespoons olive oil, divided

2 medium onions, peeled and thinly sliced

1 pound bulk spicy sausage

4 cloves garlic, peeled and crushed

2 pounds tomatoes, diced

16 ounces clam juice

2 cups chicken broth

1 cup dry vermouth

2½ cups uncooked rice

2 teaspoons coriander powder

½ teaspoon ground cumin

1 teaspoon saffron

¼ teaspoon ground white pepper

¼ teaspoon kosher salt

1 pound firm whitefish, cubed

1 pound shrimp

1 pound fresh mussels, scrubbed and rinsed

1 pound fresh clams, scrubbed and rinsed

1 large green bell pepper, seeded and diced

1 cup fresh green peas

1. Spray a 4–5-quart slow cooker with nonstick olive oil spray.

2. Heat 1 tablespoon olive oil in a large skillet over low heat. Sauté the onions and sausage until the sausage is crumbled and browned (about 10 minutes), then drain and transfer to the slow cooker.

3. Stir in garlic, tomatoes, clam juice, broth, vermouth, rice, coriander, cumin, saffron, white pepper, and salt.

4. Cover and cook on low for 4 hours.

5. Heat the remaining olive oil in a separate large skillet over low heat. Sauté the fish and shrimp in oil for 6 minutes. Transfer to the slow cooker, and add the mussels and clams. Stir in the green pepper and peas.

6. Cover and cook on low for 1 hour.

CHAPTER 7

Peas, Beans, and Lentils

Split Pea Soup

6 strips bacon, diced

2 celery stalks, finely diced

3 large carrots, peeled

1 large sweet onion, peeled and diced

2 cups dried split peas, drained and rinsed

4 cups chicken broth

3 cups water

2 large potatoes, peeled and diced

1 smoked ham hock

4 ounces smoked sausage or ham, diced

¼ teaspoon salt

¼ teaspoon freshly ground black pepper

1. Add the bacon and celery to a slow cooker; cover and cook on high while you prepare the carrots. Grate half of one of the carrots and dice the remaining carrots. Add the grated carrot and diced onion to the slow cooker; stir to mix them in with the bacon and celery. Cover and cook on high for 30 minutes or until the onions are translucent.

2. Add the diced carrots, split peas, broth, water, potatoes, ham hock, and smoked sausage or ham to the slow cooker. Cover and cook on low for 8 hours or until the peas are soft. Use a slotted spoon to remove the ham hock; remove the meat from the bone and return it to the slow cooker. Taste for seasoning and add salt and pepper if needed.

Slow Cooker Suggestions

This is a soup that can be enhanced by adding ½ cup of pork stock instead of that much of the water.

Simple Split Pea Soup

SERVES 6

2 cups dried green split peas

Water, as needed

6 cups Vegetable Stock (see recipe in Chapter 2)

2 medium potatoes, peeled and diced

2 large carrots, peeled and chopped

3 celery stalks, chopped

2 cloves garlic, peeled and minced

1 teaspoon ground cumin

1 teaspoon dried thyme

1 bay leaf, dried

1 teaspoon salt

1. Rinse the green split peas; soak overnight in enough water to cover them by more than 1". Drain.
2. In a 4-quart slow cooker, add all ingredients; cook over low heat for 6–8 hours.
3. Let the soup cool slightly, then remove the bay leaf. Process in a blender, or use an immersion blender, until smooth.

Basic Bean Soup

SERVES 8

1 (16-ounce) bag dried mixed beans, or 2¼ cups cooked beans

1 (14.5-ounce) can diced tomatoes, with juice

6 cups vegetable broth

2 cups peeled and finely diced carrots

1½ cups finely diced celery

1 cup peeled and finely chopped onions

2 tablespoons tomato paste

1 teaspoon Italian seasoning

½ teaspoon ground black pepper

1 teaspoon kosher salt

1. If using dried beans, soak them according to package directions. Rinse and place in a 4-quart or larger slow cooker.
2. Add remaining ingredients to the slow cooker.
3. Cover and cook on high for 5–6 hours or on low for 10–12 hours until the beans are tender.

Split Pea Soup with Fried Paneer

2 cups split peas (soaked overnight), or 2 (14-ounce) cans

4 cups water

¼ teaspoon salt

1 teaspoon turmeric

1½ tablespoons cooking oil

1 cup paneer cubes

1 tablespoon butter

1 teaspoon mustard seeds

1 tablespoon coriander powder

1 teaspoon ground cayenne pepper

½ cup fried brown onions

1. Drain the water in which the split peas were soaked (or if using canned split peas, drain the water from the can).

2. Add the peas to a 4–5-quart slow cooker along with 4 cups of water. Add the salt and turmeric. Cover and cook on high for 1 hour and then on low for 3–4 hours or until they are cooked through.

3. Heat the cooking oil in a skillet. Pan-fry paneer cubes on medium-high heat until they turn golden brown on all sides. Place the paneer on a paper towel to absorb the extra oil. Set aside.

4. Heat the butter in a tempering pan. Turn the heat off; add mustard seeds, coriander powder, and cayenne pepper. Cook for 30 seconds. Transfer this mixture (*tadka*) to the slow cooker. Stir well.

5. Serve the soup, while hot, into serving bowls. Add fried brown onions and 4 or 5 cubes of paneer per bowl and serve.

Baked Beans Soup

SERVES 6

2 (16-ounce) cans baked beans

1 tablespoon molasses

1 tablespoon brown sugar

6 strips bacon, diced

1 large sweet onion, peeled and diced

1 (15-ounce) can stewed tomatoes

1 (2-pound) chuck roast

¼ teaspoon salt

¼ teaspoon freshly ground black pepper

1. Add the baked beans, molasses, brown sugar, bacon, onion, and stewed tomatoes to the slow cooker; stir to mix.

2. Trim the beef of any fat and cut it into 1" cubes. Add to the slow cooker and stir it into the beans. Cover and cook on low for 8 hours or until the beef is tender. Taste for seasoning; add salt and pepper if needed.

Black Bean Soup

SERVES 8

3 slices turkey bacon

1 teaspoon canola oil

1 medium onion, peeled and diced

1 habanero pepper, seeded and minced

3 cloves garlic, peeled and minced

1 celery stalk, diced

1 large carrot, peeled and diced

2 (15-ounce) cans black beans, drained and rinsed

3 cups Chicken Stock (see recipe in Chapter 2)

1. Cook the turkey bacon in a nonstick skillet until crisp. Drain on paper towel–lined plates. Crumble the bacon into small pieces.

2. Heat the oil in a nonstick skillet. Add the onions, habaneros, garlic, celery, and carrot. Sauté until the onions are soft, about 2–4 minutes.

3. Put the beans, onion mixture, and bacon crumbles into a 4-quart slow cooker. Add the stock and stir. Cook on low for 8–10 hours or on high for 4 hours.

Lentil and Barley Soup

1 medium onion, peeled and coarsely chopped

3 cloves garlic, peeled and chopped

1½ pounds lamb bones

8 cups water

½ teaspoon kosher salt

2 bay leaves, dried

¼ teaspoon ground black pepper

1 cup brown lentils, rinsed

½ cup pearl barley

1 bunch fresh parsley leaves, coarsely chopped

1. Spray a 4–5-quart slow cooker with nonstick olive oil cooking spray.
2. Combine the onion, garlic, bones, water, salt, bay leaves, and pepper in the slow cooker. Stir in the lentils and barley.
3. Cover and cook on low for 4–5 hours. Remove the bay leaves and lamb bones.
4. Top individual servings of soup with parsley.

White Bean and Barley Soup

2 (15-ounce) cans great northern beans, drained and rinsed

½ cup pearl barley

½ onion, peeled and diced

2 large carrots, peeled and diced

2 cloves garlic, peeled and minced

¼ cup fresh parsley leaves, chopped

2 sprigs fresh thyme

6 cups Vegetable Stock (see recipe in Chapter 2)

1½ teaspoons salt

1. In a 4-quart slow cooker, add all ingredients; cover and cook on low for 6–8 hours.
2. Remove the sprigs of thyme before serving.

Red Lentil Soup

2 cups red lentils

3 tablespoons olive oil

1 small onion, peeled and sliced

1½ teaspoons peeled and minced fresh gingerroot

2 cloves garlic, peeled and minced

6 cups Vegetable Stock (see recipe in Chapter 2)

Juice of 1 lemon

½ teaspoon paprika

1 teaspoon ground cayenne pepper

1½ teaspoons salt

1. Rinse the lentils carefully and sort through the bunch to remove any dirt or debris.

2. In a sauté pan, heat the olive oil over medium heat then sauté the onion, ginger, and garlic for 2–3 minutes.

3. In a 4-quart slow cooker, add the lentils, sautéed vegetables, and all remaining ingredients; cover and cook on low for 6–8 hours. Add more salt, if necessary, to taste.

Creamy Chickpea Soup

SERVES 6

1 small onion, peeled and diced

2 cloves garlic, peeled and minced

2 (15-ounce) cans chickpeas, drained and rinsed

5 cups Vegetable Stock (see recipe in Chapter 2)

1 teaspoon salt

½ teaspoon ground cumin

Juice of ½ lemon

1 tablespoon olive oil

¼ cup fresh parsley leaves, chopped

1. In a 4-quart slow cooker, add all ingredients except for the lemon juice, olive oil, and parsley; cover and cook over low heat for 4 hours.

2. Allow to cool slightly, then process the soup in a blender or using an immersion blender.

3. Return the soup to the slow cooker then add the lemon juice, olive oil, and parsley, and heat on low for an additional 30 minutes.

Dandelion and White Bean Soup

1 teaspoon olive oil

2 large red onions, peeled and chopped

3 large carrots, peeled and diced

3 celery stalks, diced

½ teaspoon freshly ground black pepper

1 clove garlic, peeled and minced

2 quarts Vegetable Stock (see recipe in Chapter 2)

1 dried bay leaf

1 cup cooked cannellini beans

¼ bunch flat-leaf parsley leaves, chopped

4 sprigs fresh thyme, leaves stripped from the stalk

2 cups fresh dandelion greens

¼ cup shredded Parmesan cheese

1. Heat the oil in a medium skillet or Dutch oven over medium heat until hot but not smoking. Add the onions, carrots, and celery and season with pepper. Sauté until softened, about 5–8 minutes. Add garlic and cook for 1 minute.

2. Place the vegetable mixture in a 4–5-quart slow cooker. Add the stock and bay leaf. Cover and cook on low heat for 3 hours.

3. Add the beans, parsley, thyme, and dandelion greens and cook for 30 minutes more.

4. Serve with shredded cheese.

Slow Cooker Suggestions

Depending on where you live, dandelion greens may be a seasonal treat. If you can't find them, substitute arugula in the soup.

Fava Bean Soup

1 cup shelled fava beans

1 small onion, peeled and diced

2 medium carrots, peeled and diced

2 Yukon Gold potatoes, peeled and diced

2 cups diced, fresh tomatoes

6 cups Vegetable Stock (see recipe in Chapter 2)

¼ cup pitted and chopped kalamata olives

½ teaspoon red pepper flakes

¼ teaspoon salt

¼ cup chopped fresh flat-leaf parsley leaves

1. Place all of the ingredients except salt and parsley in a 6-quart slow cooker. Cover and cook on low heat for 4 hours.

2. Before serving, season with salt and garnish with fresh parsley.

White Bean Ragout

2 tablespoons olive oil

1 medium onion, peeled and diced

5 cloves garlic, peeled and minced

2 (15-ounce) cans navy beans, drained

1 (14.5-ounce) can diced tomatoes

3 cups water

¼ cup tomato paste

½ cup chopped fresh parsley leaves

2 tablespoons chopped fresh sage leaves

¼ teaspoon salt

⅛ teaspoon ground black pepper

1. Add the olive oil to a 4-quart slow cooker and sauté the onion on high heat 3–5 minutes. Add the garlic and sauté for 1 minute more.

2. Add the navy beans, tomatoes, water, tomato paste, parsley, sage, salt, and black pepper, and cook on low heat for 4 hours.

White Bean and Tomato Stew

1 (15-ounce) can cannellini beans, drained

4 cups Vegetable Stock (see recipe in Chapter 2)

1 tablespoon vegetable oil

1 teaspoon salt

2 cloves garlic, peeled and minced

½ teaspoon dried sage

¼ teaspoon dried thyme

½ teaspoon ground black pepper

1 cup diced tomato

1. In a 4-quart slow cooker, add all ingredients except for tomato. Cover and cook on low heat for 5–6 hours.
2. Add the tomato; stir and cook for an additional 30 minutes.

Slow Cooker Suggestions

Beans are an easy and delicious way to provide protein to a vegetarian or vegan diet. They are also low in fat and a good source of fiber. Cannellini, great northern, and navy are all types of white beans. Each has its own unique flavor. Cannellini are the largest, and have an earthy flavor.

White Bean Cassoulet

1 pound dried cannellini beans

2 cups boiling water

1 ounce dried porcini mushrooms

2 leeks

1 teaspoon canola oil

2 parsnips, peeled and diced

2 large carrots, peeled and diced

2 celery stalks, diced

½ teaspoon ground fennel seed

1 teaspoon dried crushed rosemary

1 teaspoon dried chervil

⅛ teaspoon cloves, ground

¼ teaspoon salt

¼ teaspoon freshly ground black pepper

2 cups Vegetable Stock (see recipe in Chapter 2)

1. The night before making the soup, place the beans in a 4-quart slow cooker. Fill with water to 1" below the top of the insert. Soak overnight.
2. Drain the beans, boil for 10 minutes, and return them to the slow cooker.
3. In a heatproof bowl, pour the boiling water over the dried mushrooms and soak for 15 minutes.
4. Slice only the white and light green parts of the leeks into ¼" rounds. Cut the rounds in half.
5. In a nonstick skillet, heat the oil; add the parsnips, carrots, celery, and leeks. Sauté for 1 minute, just until the color of the vegetables brightens.
6. Add to the slow cooker along with the spices. Add the mushrooms, their soaking liquid, and the stock; stir.
7. Cook on low for 8–10 hours.

CHAPTER 8

Potatoes, Squash, and Root Vegetables

Ham and Potato Soup

½ cup diced celery

½ cup peeled and diced onion

1 tablespoon olive oil

3½ cups peeled and diced potatoes (about 2 large russet potatoes)

1¼ cups diced cooked ham

5 cups gluten-free chicken broth

½ teaspoon salt

½ teaspoon ground white pepper

3 tablespoons sliced green onions

¼ cup shredded Cheddar cheese

1. In a large skillet, sauté celery and onion in olive oil until softened, about 3–4 minutes. Add to a greased 4-quart slow cooker.
2. Add potatoes, ham, broth, salt, and pepper to the slow cooker. Cover and cook on high for 4 hours or on low for 6–8 hours, until potatoes are very tender.
3. Ladle the soup into bowls and garnish with green onions and Cheddar cheese.

Baked Potato Soup

1 onion, peeled and sliced

4 medium russet potatoes, peeled and cubed

5 cups water

¼ teaspoon salt

½ teaspoon ground white pepper

¼ cup shredded sharp Cheddar cheese

3 tablespoons reduced-fat sour cream

2 strips turkey bacon, cooked and crumbled

⅓ cup diced green onions

1. Place the onions, potatoes, water, salt, and pepper into a 4-quart slow cooker. Cook on low for 7 hours.
2. Purée using an immersion blender or purée in batches in a blender. Stir in the cheese, sour cream, bacon crumbles, and green onion.

Tuscan Potato, Kale, and Sausage Soup

1 tablespoon olive oil

3 slices bacon, diced

1 pound Italian sausage, cut into bite-sized pieces

1 medium onion, peeled and chopped

2 cloves garlic, peeled and minced

3 tablespoons white wine

2 large russet potatoes, peeled and diced

4 cups gluten-free chicken broth

¼ teaspoon red pepper flakes

½ teaspoon salt

½ teaspoon ground black pepper

2 cups chopped fresh kale

1 cup heavy cream

1. In a large skillet heat the olive oil and cook the bacon and sausage until crisp and fat has been rendered, about 5 minutes. Remove the bacon and sausage and add to a greased 4-quart slow cooker.

2. Sauté the onion and garlic in the bacon fat until softened, 3–5 minutes.

3. Deglaze the pan with wine. Scrape the pan to remove all bits of vegetables and meat. Add all of the pan contents to the slow cooker.

4. Add potatoes, chicken broth, pepper flakes, salt, and ground pepper. Cover and cook on high for 4 hours or on low for 8 hours, until potatoes are very tender.

5. An hour before serving stir in the kale and the cream. Continue to cook for 45 minutes to an hour on high heat until the kale has softened and the cream is warmed through. Be careful not to overcook at this point as the cream can curdle and separate if heated for too long.

Potato Soup

4 strips bacon

1 small carrot, peeled and grated

½ celery stalk, finely diced

1 large sweet onion, peeled and diced

1 (4-ounce) cooked ham steak, diced

4 slices Canadian bacon

4 large potatoes, peeled and diced

5 cups chicken broth

¼ teaspoon salt

¼ teaspoon freshly ground black pepper

1. Cut the bacon into 1" pieces and add it to a slow cooker along with the carrot, celery, and onion. Cover and cook on high for 15 minutes.

2. Stir in the diced ham. Cut the Canadian bacon into bite-sized pieces and stir into the vegetables. Cover and cook on high for 15 more minutes or until the fat begins to render from the bacon and the onion is translucent.

3. Stir the diced potatoes into the onion mixture. Cover and cook on high for 15 more minutes. Add the broth, salt, and pepper; reduce the heat setting to low, cover, and cook for 4 hours or until the potatoes are cooked through.

Slow Cooker Suggestions

Once the potatoes are cooked through, add 1 cup heavy cream, 4 ounces of cream cheese cut into cubes, and 1 cup (4 ounces) grated medium or sharp Cheddar cheese to the slow cooker. Stirring occasionally, cover and cook on low for 30 minutes or until the cheeses are melted and can be stirred into the soup.

Creamy Potato Soup

6 russet potatoes, peeled and diced

2 medium onions, peeled and diced

2 carrots, peeled and finely diced

2 celery ribs, washed and finely diced

6 cups gluten-free chicken broth

1 teaspoon dried basil

½ teaspoon salt

½ teaspoon ground white pepper

¼ cup brown rice flour

1½ cups half-and-half

1. Add potatoes, onions, carrots, celery, broth, basil, salt, and pepper to a greased 4–6-quart slow cooker. Cover and cook on high for 4 hours or on low for 8 hours.

2. One hour prior to serving, add the brown rice flour and the half-and-half to a medium bowl and whisk together. Set aside.

3. Using a potato masher, roughly mash the potatoes in the slow cooker until they give the soup a creamy texture.

4. Stir the half-and-half mixture into the potato soup.

5. Cover and continue to cook for 45 minutes to an hour on high heat until the cream has been heated through and the soup has thickened slightly.

Leek, Potato, and Carrot Potage

SERVES 6

4 cups sliced leeks

4 large russet potatoes, peeled and cubed

2 large carrots, peeled and diced

5 cups water

¼ teaspoon salt

½ teaspoon ground white pepper

1. Place all ingredients into a 4-quart slow cooker. Cook on low for 7 hours.

2. Purée using an immersion blender or purée in batches in a blender. Serve piping hot.

Potato-Leek Soup

SERVES 6

2 tablespoons butter or vegan margarine

2 small leeks (white and light green parts only), chopped

3 large russet potatoes, peeled and diced

4 cups Vegetable Stock (see recipe in Chapter 2)

½ cup white wine

½ cup water

1 teaspoon salt

1 teaspoon ground black pepper

¼ teaspoon dried thyme

1. In a sauté pan over medium heat, melt the butter or vegan margarine then add the leeks. Cook until softened, about 5 minutes.

2. In a 4-quart slow cooker, add the sautéed leeks, potatoes, stock, wine, water, salt, pepper, and thyme. Cover and cook over low heat 6–8 hours.

3. Allow soup to cool slightly, then use an immersion blender or traditional blender to process until smooth.

Potato and Lentil Stew

2 tablespoons olive oil

1 onion, peeled and diced

2 carrots, peeled and sliced

2 celery stalks, chopped

3 cloves garlic, peeled and minced

½ pound potatoes, peeled and chopped into bite-sized pieces

1 pound dried green lentils

4 cups water

4 cups Vegetable Stock (see recipe in Chapter 2)

1 tablespoon soy sauce

1 bay leaf, dried

½ teaspoon salt

⅛ teaspoon ground black pepper

1. Add the olive oil to a 4-quart slow cooker and sauté the onion, carrot, and celery on high heat for 3–5 minutes. Add the garlic and sauté for 1 minute more.

2. Add the rest of the ingredients and cook on low heat for 6 hours.

Sweet Potato and Cranberry Stew

2 tablespoons olive oil

1 onion, peeled and chopped

3 cloves garlic, peeled and minced

2 teaspoons turmeric

1 teaspoon curry powder

1 teaspoon ground cumin

1 teaspoon ground cinnamon

¼ teaspoon ground nutmeg

4 sweet potatoes, peeled and cut into bite-sized cubes

2 cups frozen cranberries

6 cups Vegetable Stock (see recipe in Chapter 2)

½ teaspoon salt

⅛ teaspoon ground black pepper

1. Add the olive oil to a 4-quart slow cooker and sauté the onion on high heat for 4–5 minutes. Add the garlic and sauté for 1 minute more.

2. Add the rest of the ingredients and cook on low heat for 6 hours.

Butternut Squash Soup

2 tablespoons butter, melted

1 medium onion, peeled and diced

1 celery stalk, thinly diced

1 butternut squash, peeled, seeded, and diced

1 small Granny Smith apple, peeled, cored, and diced

2 (3") cinnamon sticks

6 whole cloves

6 allspice berries

6 cups Chicken Stock (see recipe in Chapter 2)

¼ teaspoon salt

¼ teaspoon freshly ground black pepper

2 tablespoons maple syrup

Freshly grated nutmeg

1. Add the butter, onion, and celery to the slow cooker. Cover and, stirring occasionally, cook on high for 30 minutes or until the onions begin to soften or are translucent. Add the diced squash (about 3 cups), apple, and cinnamon sticks. Place the cloves and allspice in a muslin cooking bag or tie them inside a piece of cheesecloth; add to the slow cooker along with the stock, salt, and pepper. Cover and cook on low for 6 hours or until the squash is tender.

2. Remove the cinnamon sticks, cloves, and allspice. Use an immersion blender to purée the soup. Taste for seasoning and adjust, adding maple syrup to taste if desired. Ladle into bowls. Grate fresh nutmeg to taste over each serving.

Slow Cooker Suggestions

Some supermarkets sell butternut squash that's already peeled and diced. Or, you can use a knife to pierce the squash several times, place it on a baking sheet, and bake it in a 350°F oven for an hour. Once it's cool enough to handle, cut it lengthwise. Scrape out and discard the seeds. Use a spoon to scrape the cooked flesh from the inside of the peel.

Butternut Squash Soup with Cilantro Chutney

1 tablespoon butter

1½ cups carrots, peeled and cut into chunks

4 celery stalks, sliced

2½ pounds butternut squash, peeled and cut into 1" chunks

1 medium-sized apple, peeled and cut into chunks

½ cup caramelized onions

1 teaspoon dried thyme

1 teaspoon ground black pepper

3 cups Chicken or Vegetable Stock (see recipes in Chapter 2)

¼ teaspoon salt

1 tablespoon olive oil

2 tablespoons cilantro chutney

1. Grease the inside of a 6-quart slow cooker with butter. Add all the ingredients *except* the oil and chutney into the slow cooker. Mix well.

2. Drizzle the olive oil and any remaining butter on top. Cover and cook for 4–5 hours on high or 9 hours on low.

3. Once the vegetables are cooked through, take them out of the slow cooker and purée using a hand blender. Drizzle some chutney on top and serve hot with fried poppadom (crisp Indian bread).

Slow Cooker Suggestions

Try to cut all the vegetables the same size. Different sizes lead to uneven cooking.

Butternut Squash and Potato Soup

SERVES 6

1 medium butternut squash, peeled and diced

1 russet potato, peeled and diced

1 large carrot, peeled and chopped

1 celery rib, sliced

1 onion, peeled and diced

4 cups Vegetable Stock (see recipe in Chapter 2)

1 cup white wine

1 bay leaf, dried

¼ teaspoon dried thyme

1½ teaspoons salt

¼ teaspoon ground nutmeg

1. Add all of the ingredients to a 4-quart slow cooker. Cover and cook over low heat for 6 hours.

2. Cool the soup slightly, then remove the bay leaf. Process in a blender or using an immersion blender.

Acorn Squash Autumn Bisque

SERVES 6

2 cups Chicken Stock (see recipe in Chapter 2)

2 medium-sized acorn squash, peeled and cut into cubes

½ cup peeled and chopped onion

½ teaspoon ground cinnamon

¼ teaspoon coriander powder

¼ teaspoon ground cumin

½ cup unsweetened coconut milk

1 tablespoon lemon juice

¼ teaspoon freshly ground black pepper

1. Combine the stock, squash, onion, cinnamon, coriander, and cumin in a 4-quart slow cooker. Cover and cook on high for 3–4 hours.

2. Blend the soup, coconut milk, and lemon juice in a food processor until smooth.

3. Season with pepper.

Pumpkin, Squash, and Sage Soup

SERVES 8

3 sprigs fresh sage

3 cups peeled and chopped, fresh pumpkin

2 cups peeled and chopped butternut squash

1 small white onion, peeled and diced

4 cups Vegetable Stock (see recipe in Chapter 2)

2 bay leaves, dried

2 teaspoons salt

½ cup unsweetened soy milk

1. Place the sage in a piece of cheesecloth and tie closed.
2. Combine all of the ingredients except for the soy milk in a 6-quart slow cooker. Cover and cook over low heat for 4–6 hours or until the vegetables are very tender.
3. Remove the sage and bay leaves, add the soy milk, and blend using an immersion blender until very smooth.

Pumpkin Bisque

SERVES 4

2 cups puréed pumpkin

4 cups water

1 cup fat-free evaporated milk

¼ teaspoon ground nutmeg

2 cloves garlic, peeled and minced

1 onion, peeled and minced

1. Place all ingredients into a 4-quart slow cooker. Stir. Cook on low for 8 hours.
2. Use an immersion blender or blend the bisque in batches in a standard blender until smooth. Serve hot.

Pumpkin Soup

1 medium sugar pumpkin, halved and seeded (seeds reserved)

1 tablespoon plus 2 teaspoons olive oil, divided

1½ teaspoons kosher salt, divided

1 teaspoon freshly ground black pepper, divided

2 quarts Vegetable Stock (see recipe in Chapter 2)

3 large leeks (white and pale green parts only), sliced

1½ teaspoons minced fresh gingerroot

1 teaspoon grated fresh lemon zest

1 teaspoon fresh lemon juice

1. Preheat oven to 375°F.
2. Wash the pumpkin seeds well, and pat them dry with paper towels. Place the seeds on a rimmed cookie sheet and toss with 1 tablespoon olive oil. Season with ½ teaspoon salt and ½ teaspoon pepper. Stir well and bake for 7–9 minutes or until light golden brown. Set aside.
3. Place the pumpkin halves, cut side up, in a baking dish, and drizzle each half with a teaspoon of olive oil. Season with remaining salt and pepper. Roast for 45 minutes to 1 hour or until the flesh is easily pierced with a knife. Let cool slightly and scoop the pumpkin flesh into a 4–5-quart slow cooker.
4. Add the stock, leeks, ginger, zest, and lemon juice.
5. Cover and cook on low for 3–4 hours.
6. Carefully ladle half of the soup into a blender and process to desired consistency. Pour the blended soup back into the slow cooker and stir well to combine.
7. To serve, divide the soup between 6 bowls and top with pumpkin seeds.

Pumpkin and Ginger Soup

SERVES 6

2 pounds pumpkin, peeled, seeded, and cut into cubes

3 cups Chicken Stock (see recipe in Chapter 2)

1 cup peeled and chopped onion

½ cup dry white wine

1 tablespoon chopped fresh gingerroot

1 teaspoon minced garlic

½ teaspoon ground cloves

¼ teaspoon freshly ground black pepper

1. In a 4-quart slow cooker, combine all ingredients except the pepper. Cover and cook on high for 4–5 hours.
2. Place the soup in a food processor and blend until smooth.
3. Season with pepper.

Pumpkin-Ale Soup

SERVES 6

2 (15-ounce) cans pumpkin purée

¼ cup peeled and diced onion

2 cloves garlic, peeled and minced

2 teaspoons salt

1 teaspoon ground black pepper

¼ teaspoon dried thyme

5 cups Vegetable Stock (see recipe in Chapter 2)

1 (12-ounce) bottle pale ale beer

1. In a 4-quart slow cooker, add the pumpkin purée, onion, garlic, salt, pepper, thyme, and stock. Stir well. Cover and cook over low heat for 4 hours.
2. Allow the soup to cool slightly, then process in a blender or with an immersion blender until smooth.
3. Pour the soup back into the slow cooker, add the beer, and cook for 1 hour over low heat.

Pumpkin Stew

6 cups Vegetable Stock (see recipe in Chapter 2)

2 cups peeled and cubed pumpkin

2 cups peeled and cubed potatoes

1 cup corn kernels

1 medium onion, peeled and diced

2 cloves garlic, peeled and minced

2 bay leaves, dried

2 tablespoons tomato paste

1½ teaspoons salt

½ teaspoon dried thyme

½ teaspoon dried parsley

In a 4-quart slow cooker, add all ingredients. Cover and cook over low heat for 8 hours. Remove bay leaves.

Celery Root Soup

2 tablespoons butter or vegan margarine

1 small leek (white and light green parts only), chopped

2 cloves garlic, peeled and minced

1 large celery root, peeled and cubed

2 medium russet potatoes, peeled and cubed

6 cups Vegetable Stock (see recipe in Chapter 2)

1½ teaspoons salt

1 teaspoon ground black pepper

1. In a large sauté pan over medium heat, melt the butter or margarine then add the leeks and sauté about 4 minutes. Add the garlic and sauté an additional 30 seconds.

2. In a 4-quart slow cooker, add the sautéed leeks and garlic, celery root, potatoes, stock, salt, and pepper. Cover and cook over low heat for 6–8 hours.

3. Let the soup cool slightly, then process in a blender or with an immersion blender until smooth.

CHAPTER 9

Vegetables

Fresh Vegetable Soup

6 cups water or chicken broth

1 large yellow onion, peeled and diced

2 leeks (white part only), rinsed and sliced

1 (28-ounce) can whole plum tomatoes, crushed

4 large carrots, peeled and diced

1 acorn squash, peeled, seeded, and diced

2 large potatoes, peeled and diced

2 (15-ounce) cans garbanzo or white beans, drained and rinsed

¼ teaspoon dried thyme

¼ teaspoon dried basil

¼ teaspoon dried marjoram

2 teaspoons dried parsley

2 celery stalks, sliced

½ cup chopped celery leaves

½ pound green beans, ends trimmed and cut into 2" pieces

½ pound zucchini, sliced

1 small cabbage, cored and shredded

¼ teaspoon salt

¼ teaspoon freshly ground black pepper

1. Add the water or broth, onion, leeks, tomatoes, carrots, acorn squash, potatoes, beans, thyme, basil, marjoram, and parsley to a slow cooker. Cover and cook on low for 6 hours or until the acorn squash and potatoes are tender.

2. Stir in the celery, celery leaves, green beans, zucchini, and cabbage. Add additional water or broth if needed. Cover and cook for 1 hour or until the newly added vegetables are cooked through. Ladle into soup bowls. Add salt and pepper as needed.

Garden Vegetable Soup

½ medium red onion, peeled and diced

1 small squash, peeled and diced

4 red potatoes, quartered and scrubbed

1 cup sliced okra

1 cup fresh corn kernels

1 cup green beans, cut into ½" pieces

6 cups Vegetable Stock (see recipe in Chapter 2)

6 ounces diced tomatoes

1½ teaspoons salt

1 teaspoon ground black pepper

In a 4-quart slow cooker, add all ingredients. Cover and cook over low heat for 6–8 hours.

Tomato Vegetable Soup

1 (28-ounce) can Italian plum tomatoes, undrained

2¼ cups Beef Stock (see recipe in Chapter 2)

1 medium onion, peeled and chopped

1 large celery stalk, sliced

1 medium carrot, peeled and sliced

1 red bell pepper, seeded and chopped

1 teaspoon lemon juice

¾ teaspoon garlic powder

Pinch red pepper flakes

¼ teaspoon freshly ground black pepper

1. Combine all the ingredients except pepper in a 4–6-quart slow cooker. Cover and cook on high for 4–5 hours.
2. Process the soup in a blender until smooth; season with pepper. Serve warm.

Hot and Sour Soup

4 cups Chicken Stock or Vegetable Stock
   (see recipes in Chapter 2)

1 (15-ounce) can straw mushrooms, drained

7 ounces cubed extra-firm tofu

8 ounces canned bamboo shoots, drained

3 tablespoons rice vinegar

2 tablespoons Chinese black vinegar

1 tablespoon garlic-chili sauce

3 tablespoons soy sauce

1 teaspoon freshly ground black pepper

1 teaspoon ground white pepper

½ teaspoon sesame oil

½ teaspoon hot chile oil

¾ cup snow peas

Place all ingredients into a 4-quart slow cooker. Stir. Cook on low for 8 hours or on high for 3½ hours.

Slow Cooker Suggestions

Tofu is low in calories, a good source of iron, and virtually fat-free. It is also a good source of protein, which makes it an attractive choice in vegetarian dishes. Extra-firm tofu is the best choice for slow cooker recipes because the solid texture holds up well during long cooking times.

Minestrone Soup

3 cloves garlic, peeled and minced

1 (14.5-ounce) can fire-roasted diced tomatoes

1 (28-ounce) can crushed tomatoes

2 celery stalks, diced

1 medium onion, peeled and diced

3 medium carrots, peeled and diced

3 cups Vegetable Stock or Chicken Stock (see recipes in Chapter 2)

2 (15-ounce) cans kidney beans, drained and rinsed

2 tablespoons tomato paste

2 tablespoons minced fresh basil leaves

2 tablespoons minced fresh oregano leaves

2 tablespoons minced fresh Italian parsley leaves

1½ cups shredded cabbage

¾ cup diced zucchini

1 teaspoon salt

½ teaspoon ground black pepper

8 ounces small cooked pasta

Add the garlic, diced and crushed tomatoes, celery, onions, carrots, stock, beans, tomato paste, basil, oregano, and parsley to a 4-quart slow cooker. Cook on low heat for 6–8 hours. Add shredded cabbage and zucchini and turn to high for the last hour. Stir in the salt, pepper, and pasta before serving.

Slow Cooker Suggestions

Anchellini, small shells, hoops, alfabeto, and ditalini are all small pasta shapes suitable for soup. For heartier soups, try bow ties or rotini. Thin rice noodles or vermicelli are better for Asian-style soups.

Simple Tomato Soup

SERVES 8

1 small sweet onion, peeled and finely diced

3 tablespoons coconut butter

3 (14.5-ounce) cans diced tomatoes

1 tablespoon honey

15 ounces Chicken Stock (see recipe in Chapter 2)

½ teaspoon lemon juice

1. In a small glass or microwave-safe bowl cook onions and coconut butter in the microwave on high for 1 minute to soften them.

2. Add onion mixture, tomatoes, honey, and Chicken Stock to a greased 4-quart slow cooker. Cook on high for 4 hours or on low for 8 hours.

3. After the cooking period is over, turn off the slow cooker. Add lemon juice to the soup. Allow the soup to cool for about 20 minutes and then blend using an immersion blender or by pouring the soup (a little at a time) into a kitchen blender.

Tomato Basil Soup

SERVES 5

2 tablespoons Earth Balance Original Buttery Spread

½ onion, peeled and diced

2 cloves garlic, peeled and minced

1 (28-ounce) can whole peeled tomatoes

½ cup Vegetable Stock (see recipe in Chapter 2)

1 bay leaf, dried

1 teaspoon salt

1 teaspoon ground black pepper

½ cup unsweetened soy milk

¼ cup sliced fresh basil leaves

1. In a sauté pan over medium heat, melt the Earth Balance, then sauté the onion and garlic for 3–4 minutes.

2. In a 4-quart slow cooker, add the onion and garlic, tomatoes, Vegetable Stock, bay leaf, salt, and pepper. Cover and cook over low heat 4 hours.

3. Allow to cool slightly, then remove the bay leaf. Process the soup in a blender or immersion blender.

4. Return the soup to the slow cooker, then add the soy milk and sliced basil; heat on low for an additional 30 minutes.

Spring Soup

3 pounds fresh asparagus

1 pound cauliflower

½ pound carrots, peeled and sliced

½ pound turnips, peeled and cut into 2" strips

½ pound string beans, cut diagonally

1 cup green peas

2 cups chicken broth

¼ teaspoon kosher salt

¼ teaspoon ground black pepper

½ cup chopped fresh cilantro leaves

1. Spray a 4–5-quart slow cooker with nonstick olive oil cooking spray. Cut 2" tips from the asparagus and the florets from the cauliflower and place in the slow cooker; set aside the asparagus stalks and cauliflower stems for use in other recipes.

2. Stir in carrots, turnips, beans, peas, broth, salt, and pepper. Cover and cook on low for 3½ hours.

3. Stir in the cilantro and cook for 30 minutes more.

Cauliflower Chowder

2 pounds cauliflower florets

2 quarts Vegetable Stock (see recipe in Chapter 2)

1 onion, peeled and chopped

3 cloves garlic, peeled and minced

1 teaspoon ground white pepper

1½ teaspoons salt

1½ cups broccoli florets

2 carrots, peeled and cut into coins

1 celery stalk, diced

1. In a 4-quart slow cooker, place the cauliflower, stock, onions, garlic, pepper, and salt; stir. Cook on low for 6 hours or until the cauliflower is fork-tender.

2. Use an immersion blender to purée the cauliflower in the slow cooker until very smooth.

3. Add the broccoli, carrots, and celery. Cook for 30 minutes or until the vegetables are fork-tender.

Cauliflower and Cheese Soup

1 (12-ounce) bag frozen cauliflower, thawed

1 small onion, peeled and diced

5 cups chicken broth

¼ teaspoon salt

¼ teaspoon freshly ground black pepper

4 ounces cream cheese, cut into cubes

1 cup (4 ounces) grated medium Cheddar cheese

1 cup heavy cream

1. Add the cauliflower, onion, broth, salt, and pepper to a slow cooker; cover and cook on low for 4 hours. Use an immersion blender to purée the soup if desired.

2. Stir in the cream cheese, Cheddar cheese, and cream. Cover and, stirring occasionally, cook on low for 30 minutes or until the soup is brought to temperature.

Wild Rice and Portobello Soup

½ medium yellow onion, peeled and diced

2 small carrots, peeled and diced

2 celery ribs, sliced

1 cup chopped portobello mushroom

½ cup uncooked wild rice

4 cups Vegetable Stock (see recipe in Chapter 2)

1 bay leaf, dried

1 sprig fresh rosemary

1 teaspoon salt

½ teaspoon ground black pepper

1. In a 4-quart slow cooker, add all ingredients. Cover and cook over low heat for 6 hours.

2. Remove the bay leaf and rosemary sprig before serving.

Chunky Mushroom Trio

2 tablespoons olive oil

1 medium onion, peeled and chopped

1 pound white button mushrooms, chopped

1 pound shiitake mushrooms, stemmed and chopped

1 pound oyster mushrooms, stemmed and chopped

3 cloves garlic, peeled and minced

½ pound red potatoes, scrubbed and chopped into bite-sized pieces

4 cups Vegetable Stock (see recipe in Chapter 2)

1 tablespoon soy sauce

½ cup red wine

1 teaspoon dried thyme

¼ teaspoon salt

⅛ teaspoon ground black pepper

1. Add the olive oil to a slow cooker and sauté the onion and mushrooms on high heat for 3–5 minutes. Add the garlic and sauté for 1 minute more.

2. Add the rest of the ingredients and cook on low heat for 3–4 hours.

Slow Cooker Suggestions

In recipes like this one, which contain a significant amount of alcohol, you shouldn't expect all of the alcohol to "cook off." If you are pregnant, cooking for a child, or just like to avoid alcohol, you may want to skip this recipe.

Wild Mushroom Ragout

2 tablespoons olive oil

1 medium onion, peeled and diced

½ pound white button mushrooms, sliced

½ pound shiitake mushrooms, stemmed and sliced

½ pound oyster mushrooms, stemmed and sliced

3 cloves garlic, peeled and minced

¼ teaspoon salt

⅛ teaspoon ground black pepper

1 tablespoon chopped fresh rosemary leaves

1 tablespoon chopped fresh sage leaves

2 cups diced tomatoes

2 cups Vegetable Stock (see recipe in Chapter 2)

1. Add the olive oil to a 4-quart slow cooker and sauté the onion and mushrooms on high heat for 4–5 minutes. Add the garlic, salt, and black pepper and sauté for 1 minute more.

2. Add the rosemary, sage, tomatoes, and Vegetable Stock and cook over low heat for 2 hours.

Slow Cooker Suggestions

Button mushrooms are a milder type of mushroom with little flavor, but they are inexpensive and can be used in combination with more flavorful varieties. Shiitake, oyster, chanterelle, and hen of the woods are more expensive varieties that have wonderful texture and flavor.

Roasted Red Pepper and Corn Soup

6 red bell peppers, halved and seeded

1 cup corn kernels

1 russet potato, peeled and chopped

½ medium white onion, peeled and diced

2 cloves garlic, peeled and minced

6 cups Vegetable Stock (see recipe in Chapter 2)

2 tablespoons white wine vinegar

2 bay leaves, dried

¼ teaspoon ground black pepper

1 teaspoon salt

2 tablespoons chopped fresh cilantro leaves

1. Preheat your oven's broiler.
2. Place the bell peppers on a baking sheet, skin side up, and broil for 15 minutes or until black spots appear. Remove and place the peppers in a paper or plastic bag. Close the bag and let it sit for 5 minutes to loosen the skins. Remove the peppers, peel off the skin, and chop.
3. Place the peppers and all remaining ingredients, except cilantro, in a 6-quart slow cooker. Cover and cook over low heat for 6 hours. Remove bay leaves when done.
4. Purée using an immersion blender or traditional blender. Add the cilantro before serving.

Stuffed Pepper Soup

SERVES
6

1½ pounds ground beef, browned and drained

3 cups seeded and diced green bell peppers

2 cups peeled and diced butternut squash

1 (28-ounce) can diced peeled tomatoes

1 (28-ounce) can tomato sauce

¾ cup honey

Seasonings of choice, (basil, thyme, oregano, onion flakes, etc.)
   to taste

1. Mix all the ingredients in a 4-quart slow cooker. Cover and cook on low for 3–4 hours or until the green peppers are cooked.
2. Turn heat to high and cook for 20–30 more minutes.

French Onion Soup

SERVES
8

4 large onions, peeled and thinly sliced

½ tablespoon butter

½ tablespoon olive oil

½ teaspoon sugar

3 tablespoons flour

2 quarts Beef Stock or Chicken Stock (see recipes in Chapter 2)

Place the onions, butter, oil, sugar, and flour into a 4-quart slow cooker. Cook on high for 40 minutes. Add the stock and reduce to low. Cook for 8 hours.

Slow Cooker Suggestions

Place 4 thin slices of Italian bread on a baking sheet. Sprinkle each with a teaspoon of shredded reduced-fat Italian mixed cheese or Swiss cheese. Bake for 10 minutes at 350°F.

Old-Fashioned Onion Soup

SERVES
8

6 tablespoons butter

6 medium onions, peeled and thinly sliced

4 cups beef broth

½ teaspoon kosher salt

½ teaspoon black peppercorns

¼ pound Parmesan cheese, grated, divided

1. Spray a 4–5-quart slow cooker with nonstick olive oil cooking spray.
2. Heat butter in a medium skillet over low heat. Slowly sauté onions in butter until browned, about 25 minutes.
3. Add onions, broth, salt, and peppercorns to the slow cooker.
4. Cover and cook on low for 3–4 hours.
5. Before serving, stir ¼ cup cheese into the soup. Set out the remainder to garnish individual servings.

Zucchini Soup

SERVES
8

4 cups sliced zucchini

4 cups Chicken Stock (see recipe in Chapter 2)

4 cloves garlic, peeled and minced

2 tablespoons lime juice

2 teaspoons curry powder

1 teaspoon dried marjoram

¼ teaspoon celery seeds

½ cup coconut milk

¼ teaspoon ground cayenne pepper

Pinch paprika

1. Combine all the ingredients, except the coconut milk, cayenne pepper, and paprika, in a 4–6-quart slow cooker and cook on high for 3–4 hours.
2. Process the soup, with the coconut milk, in a blender until combined.
3. Season with cayenne pepper. Serve warm, and sprinkle with paprika.

Rustic Cabbage Soup

SERVES 6

2 tablespoons olive oil

1 medium white onion, peeled and sliced

½ head cabbage, shredded

2 russet potatoes, peeled and diced

1 celery stalk, sliced

1 carrot, peeled and sliced

2 tomatoes, diced

5 cups Vegetable Stock (see recipe in Chapter 2)

¼ teaspoon salt

¼ teaspoon ground black pepper

1. Heat the olive oil in a small sauté pan over medium-low heat. Add the onions and sauté until softened, about 5 minutes, then transfer to an 8-quart slow cooker.
2. Add all remaining ingredients to the slow cooker except for salt and pepper. Cover and cook on low heat for 8 hours.
3. Add salt and pepper before serving.

Savory Beet Soup

SERVES 8

2 tablespoons olive oil

2 cloves garlic, peeled and minced

2 shallots, peeled and diced

4 beets, peeled and chopped

1 Yukon Gold potato, peeled and chopped

4 cups Vegetable Stock (see recipe in Chapter 2)

½ teaspoon dried thyme

½ teaspoon ground black pepper

¼ teaspoon salt

1. Heat the olive oil in a sauté pan over medium-low heat. Add the garlic and shallots and sauté for 2 minutes. Transfer to a 6-quart slow cooker.
2. Add the beets, potato, Vegetable Stock, thyme, and pepper. Cover and cook over low heat for 6 hours or until beets and potatoes are very tender.
3. Use an immersion blender or traditional blender to purée. Season with salt.

Carrot-Coconut Soup

2 tablespoons olive oil

½ medium onion, peeled and diced

3 cloves garlic, peeled and minced

1 pound carrots, peeled and chopped

3 cups Vegetable Stock (see recipe in Chapter 2)

1 stalk fresh lemongrass, sliced

1 tablespoon soy sauce

1 lime, juiced

1 cup coconut milk

¼ teaspoon salt

¼ cup chopped fresh basil leaves

1. Heat the olive oil in a sauté pan over medium-low heat. Add the onion and sauté until translucent, or about 5 minutes. Add the garlic and sauté for an additional 30 seconds.

2. Place the cooked onion and garlic, carrots, Vegetable Stock, lemongrass, soy sauce, and lime juice into a 6-quart slow cooker. Cover and cook on low heat for 4–6 hours or until carrots are very tender.

3. Add the coconut milk, then use an immersion blender or traditional blender and purée the soup until very smooth. Season with salt and top with fresh chopped basil.

Slow Cooker Suggestions

Coconut milk varies in thickness and fat content. Some are quite thin, and others are more like cream than milk. Most brands of canned coconut milk are very similar, but you can usually see the percentage of coconut milk to water in the list of ingredients to help you select the level of thickness you are looking for.

Creamy Broccoli Soup

6 cups broccoli florets

2 medium russet potatoes, peeled and diced

½ medium onion, peeled and chopped

4 cups Vegetable Stock (see recipe in Chapter 2)

2 tablespoons Earth Balance Original Buttery Spread

2 tablespoons flour

1 cup unsweetened soy milk

¼ teaspoon salt

1. Place the broccoli, potatoes, onion, and Vegetable Stock in a 6-quart slow cooker. Cover and cook over low heat for 6–8 hours or until the potatoes are very tender.

2. Use an immersion blender or traditional blender to purée the soup until smooth.

3. Heat the Earth Balance in a small saucepan over low heat. Once melted, add the flour and stir to form a roux. Slowly add the soy milk and whisk until smooth.

4. Add the milk mixture to the soup, stir until well combined, heat, and season with salt.

Slow Cooker Suggestions

Broccoli fares better during cooler months than it does during hot summer days. Depending on where you live, broccoli is typically at its best during the fall and winter.

Texas Stew

2 tablespoons olive oil

1 (12-ounce) package frozen veggie crumbles

1 (15-ounce) can pinto beans, drained

1 (14.5-ounce) can diced tomatoes

1 (12-ounce) package frozen corn

½ onion, peeled and diced

½ green bell pepper, seeded and diced

4 cups Vegetable Stock (see recipe in Chapter 2)

1 teaspoon salt

1. Heat the olive oil in a sauté pan over medium heat, and cook the frozen veggie crumbles until browned, about 10 minutes.

2. In a 4-quart slow cooker, add the cooked veggie crumbles and all other ingredients; cover and cook on low heat for 4–6 hours.

Super Greens Stew

2 cups chopped kale

2 cups chopped Swiss chard

1 (15-ounce) can chickpeas, drained

¼ onion, peeled and diced

1 carrot, peeled and sliced

2 cloves garlic, peeled and minced

6 cups Vegetable Stock (see recipe in Chapter 2)

1½ teaspoons salt

½ teaspoon ground black pepper

1 sprig fresh rosemary

½ teaspoon dried marjoram

In a 4-quart slow cooker, add all ingredients. Cover and cook on low heat for 6 hours. Remove rosemary sprig before serving.

Gumbo Z'Herbes

½ cup olive oil

1 onion, peeled and chopped

1 green bell pepper, seeded and chopped

2 celery stalks, chopped

4 cloves garlic, peeled and minced

½ cup flour

4 cups Vegetable Stock (see recipe in Chapter 2)

2 cups chopped okra

½ teaspoon dried thyme

½ teaspoon dried oregano

1 teaspoon salt

½ teaspoon ground black pepper

¼ teaspoon red pepper flakes

6 cups cooked white rice

1. Add the olive oil to a 4-quart slow cooker and sauté the onion, bell pepper, and celery on high heat for 4–5 minutes. Add the garlic and sauté for 1 minute more.

2. Slowly stir in the flour with a whisk and create a roux. Pour in the Vegetable Stock and continue to whisk to remove all lumps.

3. Add the rest of the ingredients, except the rice, and cook on high heat for 3–4 hours. Serve over the cooked white rice.

Slow Cooker Suggestions

The base of some of New Orleans's most well-known dishes is referred to as the "holy trinity." It contains equal parts onion, bell pepper, and celery.

Okra Gumbo

½ cup vegetable oil

½ cup flour

1 white onion, peeled and diced

1 bell pepper, seeded and diced

4 cloves garlic, peeled and minced

4 cups water

2 cups Vegetable Stock (see recipe in Chapter 2)

1 tablespoon vegan Worcestershire sauce

1 (16-ounce) package frozen chopped okra

1 tablespoon Cajun seasoning

1 bay leaf, dried

2 teaspoons salt

2 teaspoons ground black pepper

1 (7-ounce) package Gardein Chick'n Strips, chopped

½ cup chopped fresh flat-leaf parsley leaves

½ cup sliced green onions

½ teaspoon filé powder

6 cups cooked white rice

1. In a sauté pan, bring the oil and flour to medium heat, stirring continuously until the roux achieves a rich brown color, at least 10 minutes.

2. In a 4-quart slow cooker, add the roux and all remaining ingredients except the rice. Cover and cook on low heat for 6 hours.

3. Once done, remove the bay leaf. Pour each serving over 1 cup of cooked rice.

Slow Cooker Suggestions

Filé (pronounced "FEE-lay") powder is made from ground sassafras leaves. It is an essential ingredient for authentic Cajun or Creole gumbo. Used to both thicken and flavor, filé powder is thought to have been first used by the Choctaw Indians from the Louisiana bayou region. It can be found in most well-stocked grocery stores.

Beer-Cheese Soup

½ cup butter or vegan margarine

½ white onion, peeled and diced

2 medium carrots, peeled and diced

2 celery ribs, diced

½ cup flour

3 cups Vegetable Stock (see recipe in Chapter 2)

1 (12-ounce) bottle beer

3 cups milk or unsweetened soy milk

3 cups Cheddar cheese or vegan Daiya Cheddar Style Shreds

1 teaspoon salt

1 teaspoon ground black pepper

½ teaspoon dry ground mustard

1. In a sauté pan over medium heat, melt the butter or vegan margarine, then sauté the onion, carrots, and celery until just softened, about 5–7 minutes. Add the flour and stir to form a roux. Let cook for 2–3 minutes.

2. In a 4-quart slow cooker, add the cooked vegetables and roux then slowly pour in the Vegetable Stock and beer while whisking.

3. Add the milk, cheese, salt, pepper, and mustard. Cover and cook on low for 4 hours.

4. Let the soup cool slightly then blend until smooth, or you can skip this step and serve chunky.

Slow Cooker Suggestions

Plain or original soy milk typically contains sugar and has a distinct flavor that will stand out in savory dishes. For these recipes, use plain unsweetened soy milk instead.

Southwest Corn Chowder

¼ cup butter or vegan margarine

1 onion, peeled and diced

1 jalapeño pepper, seeded and minced

1 cup diced tomato

2 medium russet potatoes, peeled and diced

2 (15-ounce) cans creamed corn

2 cups water

2 cups unsweetened soy milk

1 teaspoon chili powder

1 teaspoon ground cumin

¼ teaspoon ground cayenne pepper

¼ teaspoon salt

¼ teaspoon freshly ground black pepper

1. In a sauté pan over medium heat, melt the butter or vegan margarine; add the onion and jalapeño and sauté for about 3 minutes.

2. In a 4-quart slow cooker, add all ingredients. Cover and cook on low heat for 6 hours.

Slow Cooker Suggestions

Some creamed corn recipes don't get their creaminess from dairy products; it's from the milky substance that comes from the cob after the kernels are removed.

Vegetable Dumpling Stew

2 tablespoons olive oil

½ large onion, peeled and diced

2 cloves garlic, peeled and minced

2 carrots, peeled and chopped

2 celery stalks, chopped

½ cup corn kernels

½ cup chopped okra

2 (14.5-ounce) cans diced tomatoes

4 cups Vegetable Stock (see recipe in Chapter 2)

¼ teaspoon dried rosemary

1 teaspoon dried parsley

¼ teaspoon dried oregano

½ teaspoon salt

¼ teaspoon ground black pepper

1 (6-ounce) package vegan refrigerated biscuits

1. In a sauté pan over medium heat, add the olive oil, onion, and garlic and sauté for 3 minutes.
2. In a 4-quart slow cooker, add all ingredients except for the biscuits. Cover and cook on low heat for 4–5 hours.
3. While the stew is cooking, flatten the biscuits with a rolling pin on a floured surface, then cut each into fourths.
4. Drop the biscuit pieces into the stew and cook for 30 more minutes.

CHAPTER 10

Chilis with Meat

Enchilada Chili

1 (2-pound) boneless beef chuck roast,
cut into bite-sized pieces

1 (15-ounce) can pinto and/or red kidney beans, drained and rinsed

1 (14.5-ounce) can diced tomatoes, undrained

1 (10.5-ounce) can condensed beef broth

1 (10-ounce) can enchilada sauce

1 large onion, peeled and chopped

2 cloves garlic, peeled and minced

1 cup water

4 tablespoons fine cornmeal or masa harina (corn flour)

2 tablespoons minced fresh cilantro leaves

1 cup (4 ounces) queso blanco or Monterey jack cheese, grated

1. Add the beef, beans, tomatoes, broth, enchilada sauce, onion, garlic, and water to a slow cooker. Cover and cook on low for 8 hours.

2. In a small bowl, whisk the cornmeal together with enough cold water to make a paste; stir some of the liquid from the slow cooker into the cornmeal paste and then whisk it into the chili. Cook and stir on high for 15–30 minutes or until the chili is thickened and the raw cornmeal taste is cooked out of the chili.

3. Top each serving with minced cilantro and grated cheese.

Slow Cooker Suggestions

To serve this chili as a dip, after Step 2, reduce the heat to low and stir in the cheese; continue to stir until cheese is melted. Reduce the heat setting to warm. Serve with baked corn tortilla chips. (According to your tastes, you may wish to increase the amount of cheese.)

Hearty Beef Chili

1 pound ground beef

1 cup chopped onion

¾ cup chopped green pepper

1 clove garlic, peeled and minced

1 (14.5-ounce) can diced tomatoes

1 (16-ounce) can pinto beans

1 (8-ounce) can tomato sauce

2 teaspoons chili powder

½ teaspoon crushed dried basil

1. Brown the ground beef and onion in a large skillet, approximately 5–6 minutes. Leave the ground beef in larger chunks when cooking, instead of breaking it down into very small pieces. Add cooked beef and onion to a greased 4-quart slow cooker.

2. Add the remaining ingredients. Cover and cook on high for 4 hours or on low for 8 hours.

Slow Cooker Suggestions

Some people prefer to use all beef in their chili. For a full beef, bean-free chili, use 2 pounds of ground beef and leave out the pinto beans. Quartered button mushrooms can also add a meaty texture to this chili.

Secret Ingredient Beef Chili

1 pound 94% lean ground beef

2 (14.5-ounce) cans diced tomatoes

¼ cup cubed mango

1 teaspoon liquid smoke

1 teaspoon chili powder

1 teaspoon ground jalapeño powder

1 teaspoon hot chili powder

1 teaspoon smoked paprika

2 (15-ounce) cans kidney beans, drained and rinsed

1 medium onion, peeled and diced

3 cloves garlic, peeled and minced

1 teaspoon ground cumin

1. Quickly sauté the beef in a nonstick skillet until no longer pink. Drain off all fat and discard it.

2. Place the beef and all the remaining ingredients in a 4-quart slow cooker. Stir. Cook on low for 8–10 hours.

Slow Cooker Suggestions

Canned beans are ready to eat directly out of the package, making them an excellent time saver. Dried beans need to be soaked or cooked before using. Properly cooked dried beans can be substituted for an equal amount of canned, but resist the temptation to use uncooked dried beans unless explicitly directed to in the recipe. They may not rehydrate properly.

Easy Turkey and Rice Chili

SERVES 4

1 pound ground turkey

¼ cup chopped onion

1 (14.5-ounce) can diced tomatoes

3 teaspoons chili powder

1 teaspoon ground cumin

1 teaspoon garlic, peeled and minced

1 (27-ounce) can kidney beans, undrained

1½ cups water

1 cup cooked white rice

1. Brown ground turkey in a large skillet for about 5–6 minutes until cooked through. Add onion and cook for 2–3 minutes until softened.
2. Place browned ground turkey and onions in a greased 4-quart slow cooker. Add the tomatoes, chili powder, cumin, garlic, kidney beans, and water. Stir to combine. Cover and cook on high for 2–3 hours or on low for 5–6 hours.
3. An hour before serving stir in the cooked rice.

Spicy Sausage Chili

SERVES 8

1½ pounds spicy chicken sausage

2 teaspoons ground cayenne pepper

1 tablespoon ground chipotle powder

1 teaspoon hot paprika

1 teaspoon hot chili powder

1 (15-ounce) can cannellini beans, drained and rinsed

1 (14.5-ounce) can tomatoes with green chilies

1 (15-ounce) can hominy

1 teaspoon ground cumin

1. Brown the sausage in a nonstick skillet. Drain off all fat.
2. Add the sausage and remaining ingredients to a 4-quart slow cooker and stir to combine and break up the hominy as needed. Cook on low for 8–10 hours.

Turkey-Tomatillo Chili

2 cups cubed tomatillos

1 green bell pepper, seeded and diced

1 onion, peeled and diced

1 teaspoon ground cayenne pepper

1 teaspoon ground cumin

1 teaspoon paprika

1 teaspoon chili powder

2 (15-ounce) cans chili beans, drained and rinsed

2 cups cubed cooked turkey breast

Place all ingredients except the turkey in a 4-quart slow cooker. Stir to mix the ingredients. Cook on low for 8 hours, and then stir in the turkey. Cook for an additional 30–60 minutes on high.

Slow Cooker Suggestions

Tomatillos, like tomatoes, are a part of the nightshade family of vegetables. They look like small tomatoes covered in a papery husk. The husk should be removed before eating. Look for tomatillos that are unblemished, slightly heavy for their size, and solid to the touch. They are most commonly green but can also be purple or yellow.

Lean Green Chili

2 (15-ounce) cans cannellini beans, drained and rinsed

1 teaspoon ground cumin

1 teaspoon ground jalapeño powder

1 jalapeño pepper, seeded and minced

2 cloves garlic, peeled and minced

1 (4-ounce) can green chilies, drained

1 (28-ounce) can tomatillos, drained

1 medium onion, peeled and diced

1 tablespoon lime juice

1 teaspoon celery flakes

1 celery stalk, diced

2 cups diced cooked chicken breast

Place all of the ingredients except the chicken in a 4-quart slow cooker. Cook on low for 8 hours. Stir in the chicken, put the lid back on, and cook for an additional hour on low. Stir before serving.

Slow Cooker Suggestions

Cube leftover cooked chicken or turkey breast and freeze in clearly marked 1- or 2-cup packages. Defrost overnight in the refrigerator before using. Cooked poultry should be added to a recipe during the last hour of cooking.

No Bean Chili

1 tablespoon canola oil

1 pound boneless pork tenderloin, cubed

1 large onion, peeled and diced

3 poblano chilies, seeded and diced

2 cloves garlic, peeled and minced

1 teaspoon ground cumin

1 teaspoon dried oregano

1 cup Chicken Stock (see recipe in Chapter 2)

1 (15-ounce) can crushed tomatoes

2 teaspoons ground cayenne pepper

1. In a large nonstick skillet, heat the oil. Add the pork, onion, chilies, and garlic. Sauté until the pork is no long visibly pink on any side. Drain off any fats or oils and discard them.

2. Pour the pork mixture into a 4-quart slow cooker. Add the remaining ingredients. Stir.

3. Cook on low for 8–9 hours.

Slow Cooker Suggestions

As a general rule, 1 tablespoon minced fresh herbs equals 1 teaspoon dried herbs. Fresh herbs can be frozen for future use. Discard dried herbs after 1 year.

Summer Chili

½ pound ground chicken

1 bulb fennel, diced

4 radishes, diced

2 celery stalks, diced, including leaves

2 carrots, peeled and cut into coin-sized pieces

1 medium onion, peeled and diced

1 shallot, peeled and diced

4 cloves garlic, peeled and sliced

1 habanero pepper, seeded and diced

1 (15-ounce) can cannellini beans, drained and rinsed

1 (12-ounce) can tomato paste

½ teaspoon dried oregano

½ teaspoon ground black pepper

½ teaspoon crushed dried rosemary

½ teaspoon ground cayenne pepper

½ teaspoon ground chipotle powder

1 teaspoon chili powder

1 teaspoon dried tarragon

¼ teaspoon ground cumin

¼ teaspoon celery seed

2 zucchini, cubed

10 Campari tomatoes, quartered

1 cup corn kernels

1. Sauté the meat in a nonstick pan until just browned. Add to a 4-quart slow cooker along with the fennel, radishes, celery, carrots, onion, shallot, garlic, habanero, beans, tomato paste, and all spices. Stir.
2. Cook on low for 6–7 hours; then stir in the zucchini, tomatoes, and corn. Cook for an additional 30 minutes on high. Stir before serving.

Super Mild Chili

1 pound ground turkey

2 (15-ounce) cans cannellini beans, drained and rinsed

1 (28-ounce) can crushed tomatoes

1 teaspoon dried oregano

½ teaspoon ground cumin

1 teaspoon mild chili powder

1 bell pepper, seeded and diced

1 Vidalia onion, peeled and diced

2 cloves garlic, peeled and minced

1. Brown the turkey in a nonstick skillet. Drain if needed.
2. Add the turkey and all of the remaining ingredients to a 4-quart slow cooker. Stir. Cook on low for 7–8 hours. Stir before serving.

Pumpkin Turkey Chili

2 red bell peppers, seeded and chopped

1 medium onion, peeled and chopped

4 cloves garlic, peeled and chopped

1 pound ground turkey, browned

1 (14.5-ounce) can pure pumpkin purée

1 (14.5-ounce) can diced tomatoes

½ cup water

1½ tablespoons chili powder

½ teaspoon ground black pepper

¼ teaspoon ground cumin

1. In a skillet over medium heat, sauté the peppers, onion, and garlic with the browned turkey for 5–7 minutes.
2. Transfer the turkey and veggies into a 4-quart slow cooker. Add the remaining ingredients. Cover and cook on low for 5–6 hours.

Fish Chili with Beans

2 tablespoons olive oil

1 large leek (white and pale green parts only), sliced

1 medium onion, peeled and diced

4 ounces firm tofu, drained and chopped

1 medium jalapeño pepper, seeded and sliced

1 medium serrano chili, seeded and sliced

1 teaspoon chili powder

¼ teaspoon ground cayenne pepper

½ teaspoon freshly ground black pepper

6 large plum tomatoes, diced

½ cup dry red wine

1 cup Fish Stock (see recipe in Chapter 2)

½ cup brewed strong coffee

1 teaspoon packed light brown sugar

1 tablespoon honey

2 cups cooked pinto, cannellini, or red kidney beans

2 pounds firm-fleshed fish (Chilean sea bass, halibut, or red snapper), sliced on the bias

1. Heat the oil in a large Dutch oven over medium-high heat until hot but not smoking. Add the leek, onion, tofu, jalapeño, and serrano to the pan. Season with the chili powder, cayenne, and black pepper. Cook until softened, about 5–8 minutes.

2. Pour the onion and tofu mixture into a 4–5-quart slow cooker. Add the tomatoes.

3. Whisk together the wine, stock, coffee, brown sugar, and honey in a small bowl. Pour into the slow cooker.

4. Cover and cook on low for 3½ hours. Stir in the beans and fish and cook for 30 minutes more.

Fiery Chicken Chili

1 pound ground chicken

3 cloves garlic, peeled and chopped

3 chipotle chilies in adobo

1 (15-ounce) can dark red kidney beans, drained and rinsed

1 (15-ounce) can black beans, drained and rinsed

1 teaspoon Worcestershire sauce

2 (14.5-ounce) cans diced tomatoes

1 (4-ounce) can diced green chilies

1 teaspoon ground cayenne pepper

1 teaspoon ground chipotle powder

1 onion, peeled and chopped

1 tablespoon habanero hot sauce

1 teaspoon paprika

1 teaspoon hot chili powder

1 teaspoon liquid smoke

1. Quickly sauté the ground chicken in a nonstick skillet until just cooked through. Drain all fat.

2. Place all ingredients in a 4-quart slow cooker. Stir. Cook on low for 8–10 hours.

Slow Cooker Suggestions

Liquid smoke is made by condensing smoke in water to form a fluid. It is found in a variety of flavors including hickory and mesquite and can be used to add the flavor of being slow-cooked over a flame without actually having to grill.

Chicken Chili Verde

½ tablespoon olive oil

2 pounds boneless, skinless chicken breast, cubed

2 (28-ounce) cans whole peeled tomatoes, undrained

1 (4-ounce) can diced green chilies, undrained

1 teaspoon dried thyme

1 teaspoon dried oregano

1 teaspoon dried basil

1 tablespoon chili powder

2 teaspoons ground cumin

1 tablespoon honey

1 large onion, peeled and minced

3 cloves garlic, peeled and minced

½ cup water

1. Heat oil in a skillet over medium heat. Add the chicken. Cook, stirring frequently, until chicken is browned on all sides, about 1–2 minutes per side. Place browned chicken in a greased 4–6-quart slow cooker.

2. Add the remaining ingredients over the chicken in the slow cooker.

3. Cover and cook on high for 3 hours or on low for 6 hours.

Cincinnati Chili

1 pound 93% lean ground beef

1 (15-ounce) can crushed tomatoes in juice

2 cloves garlic, peeled and minced

1 onion, peeled and diced

1 teaspoon ground cumin

1 teaspoon cocoa

2 teaspoons chili powder

½ teaspoon whole cloves

1 tablespoon apple cider vinegar

1 teaspoon ground allspice

½ teaspoon ground cayenne pepper

1 teaspoon ground cinnamon

1 tablespoon Worcestershire sauce

¼ teaspoon salt

1. In a nonstick skillet, quickly sauté the beef until it is no longer pink. Drain all fat and discard it.

2. Place all ingredients—including the beef—in a 4-quart slow cooker. Stir. Cook on low for 8–10 hours.

Slow Cooker Suggestions

Even though it is not aesthetically necessary to brown the meat when making chili, sautéing meat before adding it to the slow cooker allows you to drain off any extra fat. Not only is it healthier to cook with less fat, your chili will be unappetizingly greasy if there is too much fat present in the meat during cooking.

California Chili

1 (15-ounce) can hominy

1 (15-ounce) can fire-roasted tomatoes with garlic

½ cup canned cannellini beans, drained and rinsed

1 teaspoon ground cumin

1 teaspoon ground jalapeño powder

2 Anaheim chilies, seeded and diced

6 cloves garlic, peeled and thinly sliced

1 medium onion, peeled and diced

1 celery stalk, diced

1 tablespoon lime juice

1 teaspoon chipotle chili powder

1 teaspoon California chili powder

2 cups diced cooked chicken breast

1. Place all of the ingredients except the chicken in a 4-quart slow cooker. Cook on low for 8 hours.
2. Stir in the chicken, cover the cooker again, and cook for an additional hour on low. Stir before serving.

Texas Firehouse Chili

1 pound cubed lean beef

2 tablespoons onion powder

1 tablespoon garlic powder

2 tablespoons Mexican-style chili powder

1 tablespoon paprika

½ teaspoon dried oregano

½ teaspoon freshly ground black pepper

½ teaspoon ground white pepper

½ teaspoon ground cayenne pepper

½ teaspoon ground chipotle powder

1 (8-ounce) can tomato sauce

1. Quickly brown the beef in a nonstick skillet. Drain off any excess grease.
2. Add the meat and all of the remaining ingredients to a 4-quart slow cooker. Cook on low up to 10 hours.

Lone Star State Chili

1 celery stalk, finely chopped

1 large carrot, peeled and finely chopped

1 (3-pound) chuck roast, cut into small cubes

2 large yellow onions, peeled and diced

6 cloves garlic, peeled and minced

6 jalapeño peppers, seeded and diced

½ teaspoon freshly ground pepper

4 tablespoons chili powder

1 teaspoon dried Mexican oregano

1 teaspoon ground cumin

1 teaspoon honey

1 (28-ounce) can diced tomatoes

1 cup beef broth

1. Add all of the ingredients to a 4–6-quart slow cooker, in the order given, and stir to combine. The liquid in your slow cooker should completely cover the meat and vegetables. If additional liquid is needed add more crushed tomatoes, broth, or some water.

2. Cover and cook on low for 8 hours. Taste for seasoning, and add more chili powder if desired.

Slow Cooker Suggestions

Wear gloves or sandwich bags over your hands when you clean and dice hot peppers. It's important to avoid having the peppers come into contact with any of your skin, or especially your eyes. As an added precaution, wash your hands (and under your fingernails) thoroughly with hot soapy water after you remove the gloves or sandwich bags.

CHAPTER 11

Vegetarian Chilis

Chili con "Carne"

SERVES 4

½ cup diced onion

½ cup diced green bell pepper

1 (12-ounce) package frozen veggie burger crumbles

2 cloves garlic, peeled and minced

1 (15-ounce) can kidney beans, drained and rinsed

2 cups Vegetable Stock (see recipe in Chapter 2)

1 tablespoon chili powder

½ tablespoon ground chipotle powder

½ tablespoon ground cumin

1 teaspoon dried thyme

1 tablespoon dried oregano

2 cups diced fresh tomatoes

1 tablespoon tomato paste

1 tablespoon cider vinegar

2 teaspoons salt

In a 4-quart slow cooker, add all ingredients. Cover and cook on low heat for 5 hours.

Shredded "Chicken" Chili

SERVES 4

½ cup diced onion

½ cup diced green bell pepper

1 (8-ounce) package MorningStar Farms Meal Starters Chik'n Strips, shredded by hand

2 cloves garlic, peeled and minced

1 (15-ounce) can kidney beans, drained and rinsed

2 cups Vegetable Stock (see recipe in Chapter 2)

1 tablespoon chili powder

½ tablespoon ground chipotle powder

½ tablespoon ground cumin

1 teaspoon dried thyme

1 tablespoon dried oregano

1 (15-ounce) can diced tomatoes, drained

1 tablespoon tomato paste

1 tablespoon cider vinegar

2 teaspoons salt

In a 4-quart slow cooker, add all ingredients. Cover and cook on low heat for 5 hours.

Five-Pepper Chili

1 onion, peeled and diced

1 jalapeño pepper, seeded and minced

1 habanero pepper, seeded and minced

1 green bell pepper, seeded and diced

1 poblano pepper, seeded and diced

2 cloves garlic, peeled and minced

2 (15-ounce) cans crushed tomatoes

2 cups diced fresh tomatoes

2 tablespoons chili powder

1 tablespoon ground cumin

½ tablespoon ground cayenne pepper

⅛ cup vegan Worcestershire sauce

2 (15-ounce) cans pinto beans

1 teaspoon salt

¼ teaspoon ground black pepper

In a 4-quart slow cooker, add all ingredients. Cover and cook on low heat for 5 hours.

Three-Bean Chili

1 (15-ounce) can pinto beans, drained

1 (15-ounce) can black beans, drained

1 (15-ounce) can great northern white beans, drained

1 onion, peeled and diced

3 cloves garlic, peeled and minced

3 cups Vegetable Stock (see recipe in Chapter 2)

1 tablespoon chili powder

½ tablespoon ground chipotle powder

½ tablespoon ground cumin

½ tablespoon paprika

1 (14.5-ounce) can diced tomatoes

1 teaspoon salt

¼ teaspoon ground black pepper

In a 4-quart slow cooker, add all ingredients. Cover and cook on low heat for 5 hours.

Sweet Potato Chili

1 red onion, peeled and diced

1 jalapeño pepper, seeded and minced

3 cloves garlic, peeled and minced

1 (15-ounce) can black beans, drained

1 sweet potato, peeled and diced

3 tablespoons chili powder

1 tablespoon paprika

1 teaspoon dried oregano

1 teaspoon ground cumin

½ teaspoon ground chipotle powder

1 (28-ounce) can diced tomatoes, drained

2 cups Vegetable Stock (see recipe in Chapter 2)

1 teaspoon salt

¼ teaspoon ground black pepper

1 lime, juiced

¼ cup chopped fresh cilantro leaves

1. In a 4-quart slow cooker, add all ingredients except the lime and cilantro. Cover and cook on low heat for 8 hours.

2. When the chili is done cooking, mix in the lime juice and garnish with the cilantro.

Slow Cooker Suggestions

Chili powder is made from grinding dried chilies and may be created from a blend of different types of chilies or just one variety. The most commonly used chilies are red peppers and cayenne peppers.

Fajita Chili

1 red onion, peeled and diced

1 jalapeño pepper, seeded and minced

3 cloves garlic, peeled and minced

1 (15-ounce) can black beans, drained

1 (14.5-ounce) can diced tomatoes, drained

1 (8-ounce) package MorningStar Farms Meal Starters Chik'n Strips, cut into bite-sized pieces

2 cups Vegetable Stock (see recipe in Chapter 2)

2 teaspoons chili powder

1 teaspoon sugar

1 teaspoon paprika

¼ teaspoon garlic powder

¼ teaspoon ground cayenne pepper

¼ teaspoon ground cumin

1 teaspoon salt

¼ teaspoon ground black pepper

In a 4-quart slow cooker, add all ingredients. Cover and cook on low heat for 5 hours.

Slow Cooker Suggestions

One way to simplify this recipe is to use a packet of fajita seasoning (sold in the international aisle in many stores) in place of the chili powder, sugar, paprika, garlic powder, cayenne pepper, cumin, salt, and black pepper.

Black Bean, Corn, and Fresh Tomato Chili

1 red onion, peeled and diced

1 jalapeño pepper, seeded and minced

3 cloves garlic, peeled and minced

1 (15-ounce) can black beans, drained

1 (15-ounce) can corn, drained

3 tablespoons chili powder

1 tablespoon paprika

1 teaspoon dried oregano

1 teaspoon ground cumin

½ teaspoon ground chipotle powder

2 cups Vegetable Stock (see recipe in Chapter 2)

1 teaspoon salt

¼ teaspoon ground black pepper

2 cups diced tomato

¼ cup chopped fresh cilantro leaves

4 tablespoons sour cream or vegan sour cream

1. In a 4-quart slow cooker, add all ingredients except tomatoes, cilantro, and sour cream. Cover and cook on low heat for 5 hours.
2. When the chili is done cooking, mix in the tomatoes and garnish with the cilantro. Top with sour cream or vegan sour cream.

Red Bean Chili

2 (15-ounce) cans red kidney beans, drained

½ cup diced onion

2 cloves garlic, peeled and minced

2 cups Vegetable Stock (see recipe in Chapter 2)

1 tablespoon chili powder

½ tablespoon ground chipotle powder

½ tablespoon ground cumin

½ tablespoon paprika

1 (14.5-ounce) can diced tomatoes

1 teaspoon salt

¼ teaspoon ground black pepper

In a 4-quart slow cooker, add all ingredients. Cover and cook on low heat for 5 hours.

Lentil Chili

SERVES
6

1 cup lentils, uncooked

1 onion, peeled and diced

3 cloves garlic, peeled and minced

4 cups Vegetable Stock (see recipe in Chapter 2)

¼ cup tomato paste

1 cup peeled and chopped carrots

1 cup chopped celery

1 (14.5-ounce) can diced tomatoes, drained

2 tablespoons chili powder

½ tablespoon paprika

1 teaspoon dried oregano

1 teaspoon ground cumin

1 teaspoon salt

¼ teaspoon ground black pepper

In a 4-quart slow cooker, add all ingredients. Cover and cook on low heat for 8 hours.

Garden Vegetable Chili

1 large onion, peeled and diced

3 cloves garlic, peeled and minced

1 large green bell pepper, seeded and chopped

2 cups chopped zucchini

1½ cups corn kernels

1 (28-ounce) can diced tomatoes

2 cups Vegetable Stock (see recipe in Chapter 2)

1 (15-ounce) can kidney beans, drained

1 (15-ounce) can pinto beans, drained

1 (15-ounce) can cannellini beans, drained

2 tablespoons chili powder

1 teaspoon ground cumin

1 teaspoon dried oregano

1 teaspoon salt

¼ teaspoon ground black pepper

In a 4-quart slow cooker, add all ingredients. Cover and cook on low heat for 6 hours.

Slow Cooker Suggestions

In the summer, bell peppers, corn, green beans, and okra are in season and would be delicious additions to this recipe. In the winter, cauliflower, parsnips, and winter squash may be in season and would be good too.

Black Bean and "Sausage" Chili

SERVES **6**

1 red onion, peeled and diced

1 jalapeño pepper, seeded and minced

2 carrots, peeled and chopped

3 cloves garlic, peeled and minced

1 (15-ounce) can black beans, drained

1 (14-ounce) package Gimme Lean Sausage, crumbled

3 tablespoons chili powder

1 tablespoon paprika

1 teaspoon dried thyme

1 teaspoon ground cumin

½ teaspoon ground chipotle powder

1 (28-ounce) can diced tomatoes, drained

2 cups Vegetable Stock (see recipe in Chapter 2)

1 teaspoon salt

¼ teaspoon ground black pepper

In a 4-quart slow cooker, add all ingredients. Cover and cook on low heat for 5 hours.

Pumpkin Chili

SERVES **6**

2 tablespoons olive oil

1 onion, peeled and diced

2 (14.5-ounce) cans diced tomatoes

1 cup Vegetable Stock (see recipe in Chapter 2)

1 pumpkin, rind and seeds removed, flesh cut into ½" chunks

1 (14-ounce) can white beans, drained

2 tablespoons chili powder

3 teaspoons ground cumin

1 teaspoon salt

½ teaspoon ground black pepper

1. Add the oil to a 4-quart slow cooker and sauté the onion on high heat for 3–5 minutes.

2. Add the rest of the ingredients and cook on low heat for 6 hours.

Summer Chili

1 bulb fennel, diced

4 radishes, diced

2 celery stalks including leaves, diced

2 carrots, peeled and cut into coin-sized pieces

1 medium onion, peeled and diced

1 shallot, peeled and diced

4 cloves garlic, peeled and sliced

1 habanero pepper, seeded and diced

1 (15-ounce) can cannellini beans, drained and rinsed

1 (12-ounce) can tomato paste

½ teaspoon dried oregano

½ teaspoon ground black pepper

½ teaspoon crushed dried rosemary

½ teaspoon ground cayenne pepper

½ teaspoon ground chipotle powder

1 teaspoon chili powder

1 teaspoon dried tarragon

¼ teaspoon ground cumin

¼ teaspoon celery seed

2 zucchini, cubed

10 Campari tomatoes, quartered

1 cup corn kernels

1. In a 4-quart slow cooker, add the fennel, radishes, celery, carrots, onion, shallot, garlic, habanero, beans, tomato paste, and all spices; stir. Cook on low for 6–7 hours.

2. Stir in the zucchini, tomatoes, and corn. Cook for an additional 30 minutes on high. Stir before serving.

Acorn Squash Chili

2 cups cubed acorn squash

2 (14.5-ounce) cans petite diced tomatoes

2 celery stalks, diced

1 medium onion, peeled and diced

3 cloves garlic, peeled and minced

2 carrots, peeled and diced

1 teaspoon mesquite liquid smoke

2 teaspoons hot sauce

1 teaspoon chili powder

1 teaspoon paprika

1 teaspoon dried oregano

1 teaspoon smoked paprika

1 (15-ounce) can kidney beans, drained and rinsed

1 (15-ounce) can cannellini beans, drained and rinsed

1 cup fresh corn kernels

1. In a 4-quart slow cooker, add all ingredients except the corn. Cover and cook for 8 hours on low.

2. Add the corn and stir. Cover and continue to cook on low for ½ hour. Stir before serving.

Southwest Vegetable Chili

1 (28-ounce) can diced tomatoes

1 (15-ounce) can red kidney beans

1 onion, peeled and chopped

1 green bell pepper, seeded and chopped

1 red bell pepper, seeded and chopped

1 zucchini, chopped

1 squash, peeled and chopped

¼ cup chopped pickled jalapeño peppers

⅛ cup chili powder

2 tablespoons garlic powder

2 tablespoons ground cumin

1 teaspoon ground chipotle powder

⅛ teaspoon dried thyme

1 teaspoon salt

¼ teaspoon ground black pepper

In a 4-quart slow cooker, add all ingredients. Cover and cook on low heat for 5 hours.

Spicy Vegetarian Chili

2 tablespoons olive oil

1½ cups chopped yellow onion

1 cup chopped red bell pepper

2 tablespoons minced garlic

2 serrano peppers, seeded and minced

1 medium zucchini, diced

2 cups frozen corn

1½ pounds portobello mushrooms (about 5 large), stemmed, cleaned, and cubed

2 tablespoons chili powder

1 tablespoon ground cumin

1¼ teaspoons salt

¼ teaspoon ground cayenne pepper

2 (14.5-ounce) cans diced tomatoes

2 (15-ounce) cans black beans

1 (15-ounce) can tomato sauce

2 cups Vegetable Stock (see recipe in Chapter 2), or water

¼ cup chopped fresh cilantro leaves

1. In a large, heavy pot, heat the oil over medium-high heat. Add the onions, bell peppers, garlic, and serrano peppers, and cook, stirring, until soft, about 3 minutes.

2. Add the softened vegetables to a greased 4–6-quart slow cooker. Add remaining ingredients, except for cilantro.

3. Cover and cook on high for 4–6 hours or on low for 8–10 hours. Stir in cilantro before serving.

Black Bean and Butternut Squash Chili

SERVES

8

2 tablespoons olive oil

1 medium sweet onion, peeled and chopped

3 cloves garlic, peeled and minced

3 tablespoons gluten-free chili powder

2 teaspoons ground cumin

2½ cups butternut squash, peeled, cooked, and cubed

2 (15-ounce) cans black beans, drained and rinsed

4 cups gluten-free vegetable broth

1 (14.5-ounce) can diced tomatoes in juice

3 cups fresh kale, washed, patted dry, chopped

1 teaspoon salt

½ teaspoon freshly ground black pepper

1. In a skillet, heat olive oil. Sauté the onion and garlic until soft, about 3–5 minutes. Add the chili powder and cumin and cook for 1–2 minutes to release the aroma of the spices. Add the onion mixture to a greased 4-quart slow cooker.

2. Add the squash, beans, broth, and tomatoes to the slow cooker. Cover and cook on high for 4 hours or on low for 8 hours.

3. An hour prior to serving, stir in the chopped kale, salt, and pepper.

Slow Cooker Suggestions

Any type of cubed winter squash (other than spaghetti squash), or even peeled and cubed sweet potatoes, would work perfectly in this vegetarian chili.

Mushroom Chili

3 portobello mushrooms, stemmed, cleaned, and cubed

1 (15-ounce) can black beans, drained and rinsed

1 onion, peeled and diced

3 cloves garlic, peeled and sliced

2½ cups diced fresh tomatoes

1 chipotle pepper in adobo, minced

½ teaspoon jalapeño hot sauce

1 teaspoon ground cumin

½ teaspoon ground cayenne pepper

½ teaspoon freshly ground black pepper

¼ teaspoon salt

Place all ingredients into a 4-quart slow cooker. Stir. Cook on low for 8 hours.

US/Metric Conversion Chart

VOLUME CONVERSIONS

US Volume Measure	Metric Equivalent
⅛ teaspoon	0.5 milliliter
¼ teaspoon	1 milliliter
½ teaspoon	2 milliliters
1 teaspoon	5 milliliters
½ tablespoon	7 milliliters
1 tablespoon (3 teaspoons)	15 milliliters
2 tablespoons (1 fluid ounce)	30 milliliters
¼ cup (4 tablespoons)	60 milliliters
⅓ cup	90 milliliters
½ cup (4 fluid ounces)	125 milliliters
⅔ cup	160 milliliters
¾ cup (6 fluid ounces)	180 milliliters
1 cup (16 tablespoons)	250 milliliters
1 pint (2 cups)	500 milliliters
1 quart (4 cups)	1 liter (about)

WEIGHT CONVERSIONS

US Weight Measure	Metric Equivalent
½ ounce	15 grams
1 ounce	30 grams
2 ounces	60 grams
3 ounces	85 grams
¼ pound (4 ounces)	115 grams
½ pound (8 ounces)	225 grams
¾ pound (12 ounces)	340 grams
1 pound (16 ounces)	454 grams

OVEN TEMPERATURE CONVERSIONS

Degrees Fahrenheit	Degrees Celsius
200 degrees F	95 degrees C
250 degrees F	120 degrees C
275 degrees F	135 degrees C
300 degrees F	150 degrees C
325 degrees F	160 degrees C
350 degrees F	180 degrees C
375 degrees F	190 degrees C
400 degrees F	205 degrees C
425 degrees F	220 degrees C
450 degrees F	230 degrees C

BAKING PAN SIZES

American	Metric
8 x 1½ inch round baking pan	20 x 4 cm cake tin
9 x 1½ inch round baking pan	23 x 3.5 cm cake tin
11 x 7 x 1½ inch baking pan	28 x 18 x 4 cm baking tin
13 x 9 x 2 inch baking pan	30 x 20 x 5 cm baking tin
2 quart rectangular baking dish	30 x 20 x 3 cm baking tin
15 x 10 x 2 inch baking pan	30 x 25 x 2 cm baking tin (Swiss roll tin)
9 inch pie plate	22 x 4 or 23 x 4 cm pie plate
7 or 8 inch springform pan	18 or 20 cm springform or loose bottom cake tin
9 x 5 x 3 inch loaf pan	23 x 13 x 7 cm or 2 lb narrow loaf or pate tin
1½ quart casserole	1.5 liter casserole
2 quart casserole	2 liter casserole

INDEX